# PHC

# FELINE LOWDOWN ON LOCKDOWN

written and illustrated
by Sarah Veness

Michael Terence
Publishing

First published in paperback by
Michael Terence Publishing in 2020
www.mtp.agency



ISBN 9781800940840



Cover image by
Sarah Veness

Cover design

# Dedication

To everyone who fears the dark:
'Don't curse the darkness – light a candle'

# March 2020

A 'purrfect pawtrait'.

# 16TH MARCH

Honestly Sarah and Celia are very ungrateful, they didn't appreciate my help or early Easter present yesterday.

Sarah was asleep in bed in the afternoon and Celia decided that the best thing to do was go to church without her. I thought she ought to go so I leapt on her from a great height and gave her a sudden awakening. I'm not sure who was more cross? Sarah shot out of bed at a speed of zero to 60mph and staggered into the car and off they went. Last night when Sarah had gone to bed, I brought them an early Easter present of a dead rabbit - you have no idea of the effort to drag it from the woods and then pull it through the cat flap. The next thing I heard was Celia screeching and running in the opposite direction. She didn't worry about waking Sarah up this time! Sarah staggered down in her pink pyjamas and bare feet to find Celia mouthing something in the breakfast room. Galvanized unwillingly into action Sarah looked at the unwanted gift and went outside, to get the garden trowel to move it. The security lights didn't come on and she couldn't find the trowel, Celia then appeared with a torch and Sarah had to go back out to find it. Trowel in hand she scooped up the rabbit and flicked it into a flowerpot, then wondered where to put it. Celia meantime was in the next room as far from the kitchen door as she could get, only moving to offer Sarah a plastic bag to put my present in. As I said before it smacked of ingratitude. When Sarah was back in bed, I attacked her toe.

# 22nd March

Last night I crept along to Sarah's bedroom and when she wasn't looking slid onto her bed, I think she was a bit sad, so I lay still and was just a comforting friend, she seemed to appreciate it.

I didn't bite her toes when she moved and kept a low profile.

At 2.10am I crept up and nuzzled her chin, I think she must have been listening to Celia (the Cat Whisperer) as she decided that perhaps I wanted to go back to my own bed. She got up and was on her way downstairs when I nipped into Celia's bedroom because I knew Celia would open the doors for me. Sarah opened all the doors and went back to bed. In the meantime, I had made myself comfortable in Celia's room. I then decided to wake Celia up to let me out.

Needless to say, Sarah went straight back to sleep and Celia didn't.

# 24TH MARCH

Today I overheard the man over the road talking to Sarah, boring stuff like gardening, and walking the dog, they stood a long way away from each other so I guess that's why their voices were louder than usual.

Anyway, I heard him say that I was a very feisty cat and that when he and the dog walked past the entrance to my house, please note 'my house', that I arched my back and looked menacing. I can look like that when I want to.

I guess I now have a reputation to live up to. I popped out into the street and looked for them and practised my menacing look.

Beware, Celia and Sarah, especially as you can't go out and I can!

# 26th March

This morning after a night on the tiles Daphne came into my bedroom to stuff things into the revolving television. I never get a good picture on it. She pointed out it's not a television, it's a washing machine. She then had the cheek to come in and disturb me a second time.

Honestly, some people can be a bit lacking in sensitivity to my needs.

I gave her one of my withering looks.

She didn't come back again so it must have worked.

This afternoon I spent a couple of hours playing with the tabby cat who doesn't seem to recognise it's my garden. Still we had a good time and Sarah was lurking in the flower beds with her camera and a gardening fork, I avoided her.

Yesterday she was skulking in the front garden and spent ages talking into that small black box that she keeps with her all the time. She was yapping away to Lesley when out of the corner of her eye she spotted me making my way into the fountain.

She bellowed at me in rather a fishwife sort of voice 'Phoebe stop it, get out of the pond at once!' Poor Lesley was nearly deafened.

Anyway, I wasn't planning on catching a fish for my supper, she was just panicking.

Today Sarah has been wittering about finishing writing her new book. She says she has just about done it. Perhaps tomorrow she will be a bit nicer to me!

# 27th March

I thought I heard the words 'Blooming cat' when Sarah looked under her bed. I really don't see what was wrong with me taking a few bites out of a cardboard storage box that she had put there.

It tasted horrible anyway so I spat the bits out and left them there so she could stick them back on. She had just hoovered her room so I know she can easily get rid of them. She said the pieces were too big for the hoover to suck up, I will wait and see.

Sarah was in the garden again weeding and she had her black box with her but it wasn't pressed to her ear, it was propped up on the hedge and a disembodied voice came out of it.

I thought that was quite frightening but she kept laughing.

She said she was listening to a play, how can you listen to a play, surely you need to be active to play? The tabby cat and I gave her a demonstration of what playing is: hide and seek is much less frightening unless another cat creeps up on you or shouts 'Meow' loudly when you're not expecting it.

I have been banished to the garden this morning after Celia came downstairs after a bath and I attacked her bare leg.

It was very out of character. I tried to explain that I mistook it for a bit of the bannister. Well it was very white, but Sarah told me that was no excuse as there are no white bannisters in the kitchen and I shouldn't scratch the bannisters anyway.

A dog would have gone off with its tail between its legs but I held my tail up high in an imperious manner as I was shown the door and told to go outside.

# 28th March

After yesterday's bad start (don't mention mistaking Celia's leg for a bannister), I spent a lot of time in the garden frolicking about and trying to put the whole incident behind me. It was a sunny afternoon and Sarah was there with her black box again. It was different disembodied voices this time, and they seemed to be talking about the 1919 Spanish flu epidemic. Sarah seemed engrossed in it and I heard her telling Celia that she is writing an article or a story, or both, about it.

I heard her talking to a man on the black box at teatime and she seemed very excited, in fact, she was nearly late for tea.

The man kindly emailed her with what Sarah called 'exciting information'. She has been tapping away making an awful clicking noise on her large grey box. I even caught her talking to herself in an animated way!

The muttering included some words which she kept repeating: West Ham, William Frederick White, Nursing, Spanish flu and Where are the biscuits?

She thinks she is a detective, but I know otherwise, but then, of course, she did know it was me who chewed the box under her bed. Suspects were limited - Dave, Daphne, Celia and me. She has never seen them eating a box but she has seen me doing it so you didn't have to be Agatha Christie to come to a conclusion.

She says she has photographic evidence, but I don't believe her!

# 29TH MARCH

Well would you believe it, no one here seems to be the slightest bit grateful for my gifts. Yesterday I deposited a dead mouse in the boot room. It was right by my food bowl. I thought that was an appropriate place to put it, in case Celia didn't want it, then I could have it for my elevensies.

I saw Celia picking it up with a dustpan and brush, I thought she would have used a plate or a bowl, there is no telling what she will do next!

To my amazement and hurt pride, she threw it in the rubbish bin, tying a knot in the black plastic sack. She then left it by the kitchen door and went off muttering about how she had to take the bag outside in her pyjamas.

The rest of the day was fairly unremarkable, Sarah said it was a bit cold for gardening.

I realised that humans cook their meat before eating it, I heard someone mention *Mouseaka.*

So, I wondered if they would like another donation, as Celia and Sarah can't go to the shops.

As they sat eating their evening meal, I brought them another gift. I thought perhaps some fresh meat might be better.

Sarah is terrified of mice and has been known to stand on a chair and scream if she saw one, but did she this time?

No, she rushed into the kitchen before she had time to think and covered the live mouse with a plastic bowl then started shouting 'I need a piece of card!'

I wondered if she was going to make a meal of it! No one had any card close to hand, so Dave came to her rescue and slid the bowl and the mouse across the kitchen floor and then out into the garden.

I had hoped to see Sarah on the kitchen table so I was very disappointed.

In the early hours of the morning, I jumped onto Sarah's bed. She woke up with a start as I walked gently up her spine; she didn't seem very appreciative of me head butting her chin either. I leapt off and hid under her bed, but the temptation to chew her box overcame me and on hearing a ripping noise, she put her hand down by the valance where I was having a quick nibble. I put my paws out to stop her but it gave my game away and she escorted me downstairs.

I tried to skedaddle into Celia's room but she was in a deep sleep so Sarah continued 'doggedly' to get me downstairs. Every sixth step I rolled over onto my back hoping she would tickle my tummy and forget what she was doing, but on this occasion, her memory was better than normal and she shut me in the boot room and went back to bed.

# 31st March

Yesterday I started the day by bringing in a shrew just for a bit of variety.

Sarah seemed very nervous when she came downstairs, she put her breakfast on the table and called my name and checked in the boot room for any fresh bodies that I may have murdered.

I felt very affronted and while she was looking for me, I had crept onto her chair. She turned around just as my tongue was poised over her yogurt and berries.

'Blooming cat' she screeched and then in a very ungainly way removed me from her chair with the words 'I hope her tongue didn't go into my breakfast, naughty cat, bad cat'.

I am a naughty cat (but nice!) and left her wondering if my shrew bated breath had touched her breakfast.

Needless to say, in these times of austerity she ate it.

I slept most of the day after my busy night hunting.

I popped out early evening, returned wet and dozed in an armchair while Dave and Daphne read their books and Celia read a magazine. Sarah was faffing about on her grey box clicking away and muttering.

Her memory seemed particularly bad, she said 'Oh no I have forgotten what I was going to say.' She doesn't even know what day it is, and if she goes to look something up on Google, by the time she has gone onto the Google page she can't remember what she wanted to look up.

I do hope she remembers to make the lemon meringue pie today - the last four evenings she has promised to make it and when she sits at the table it occurs to her that they will need an alternative pudding.

# April 2020

Occasionally I look as if butter wouldn't melt in my mouth.

# April 1st

Well I guess the main question you are asking yourself today is 'Did Sarah remember to make the lemon meringue pie?' Well, I will put you out of your misery - the answer is NO!

But all was not lost as Celia remembered and she made sure Sarah produced this pudding.

There will now be a *paws* in transmission as Sarah goes off to hunt for the piece of paper she jotted her notes on yesterday.

This could take quite a while as she has lots of pieces of paper in her bedroom and will she remember what she had gone up for? Will she come down with a copy of her family tree that she is working on during the lockdown? Not much of a tree in my opinion as she hasn't included me.

I can hear her coming downstairs humming a song from The Sound of Mewsick, well it's not so much the song that's the problem, it's the singer. She said she's not tone deaf (I disagree) but that she's tone dumb. She can hear it's out of tune but can't do anything about it!

Normal service will now be resumed, I left a dead shrew in the kitchen, well that's where the food gets prepared. It was removed. Last night I brought in a live mouse, but Dave was on my case and swiftly ushered it back out into the garden. Some people say it's unlucky to enter a house by one door and leave by another. It was lucky for the mouse but not for me.

Celia and Sarah now go for a walk every day in the woods, I'm not sure how much good it does them, but when they got back Sarah mistook me for her slippers. (Should have gone to

Specsavers!) Having realised her mistake, she then proceeded to put them on the wrong feet and had a very puzzled look on her face. Thank goodness she found out before trying to ram me onto her feet, I would have let her know immediately.

Thank you for all the likes on Facebook and the fan mail which Sarah reads me from around the world. She has now got her glasses on! Thank you, Lily, Henry, Charlie, Horrible Harry, Minette, Lara, Odette and Cookie.

Sarah took a photo of the lemon meringue pie, Celia hastily scooped up the remains and put it in the fridge saying 'I wouldn't want Phoebe to get her paws on it.'

Honestly, I thought Celia was a cat whisperer, it wasn't my paws that would be the problem it would be my tongue.

I'd better go now and see what's happening in the big wide world and leave Sarah to her muttering and tapping her grey box before she does my head in.

# 2ND APRIL

This morning Sarah gingerly put her head around the door to see if I had left her any gifts.

She and Celia are very ungrateful and don't deserve any more presents at all, but I am very generous by nature.

Yesterday I spent a lot of the day snoozing or pretending to snooze and listening in to their conversations.

Sarah spent the morning writing my update and thinking of new ways to make it more interesting. She did a lot of laughing and kept apologising to Daphne who was working on her grey box too.

Sarah has got a new programme on her grey box for doing things with photographs, heaven help us all!

In the afternoon she decided to do some gardening, well that's what she called it and dragged me unceremoniously out with her, muttering about how I should be awake in the day and sleep at night, she's not a cat understanderer. But I will train her over time, sadly she's a slow learner.

She was out in what she calls the greenhouse. I have no idea why it's called that, there's nothing green about it, I think it should be called the clear house, or in her case the grubby window house.

She collected from there a pile of small orange tubs and went to wash them in the boot roomwhich in case hadn't realised is my bedroom.

She marched out purposefully to the grubby window house and discovered that I had decided to sit in the largest cat litter tray, you have ever seen. 'Get out of there Phoebe!' she screeched.

I did a little straining movement just to wind her up.

She told me it wasn't a litter tray but her potting tray.

Shoved out I went back inside for an uninterrupted snooze.

Having sown her seeds, she came back and found a message on her black box from the credit card fraud department.

Panic, you should have seen her panic, she got all shouty and panicked some more.

She had a very trying time trying to get through to someone who could help her. She didn't ring the number that had been left on the answerphone as it wasn't the same number on their website.

They kept giving her a list of options but her memory was so bad that she had to listen to it over and over until she could remember the next step which she had to repeat into her black box. She also said some words which I would be too embarrassed to repeat.

It turned out ok in the end, they rung her and put a stop on her card due to unusual activity. There was no unusual activity, unless you class me going out in daylight as not the norm.

Sarah asked me if I had heard of the garlic diet - I hadn't - so she went on to tell me that you don't lose much weight, but from a distance, your friends think you look thinner! Next time she goes out for a walk she will see if anyone looks thinner than before the lockdown started.

Must go now as a man rang our doorbell and left a parcel by the front door, I wonder what's in it. I do hope it's for me.

# 3RD APRIL

Sarah seems a little grumpy this morning, she got a letter marked PRIVATE & CONFIDENTIAL.

She read it to me and it says she must stay in for 12 weeks and not even go for her daily walk with Celia.

The sentence that hit me was 'try to keep 2 metres away from others and encourage them to sleep in a different bed where possible'. I like sneaking up and sleeping on her bed if she has inadvertently left the door open!

At least she can come out in the garden with me.

On a more cheerful note, lots of parcels came yesterday, she has got a new box that she talks to people on. This is a white box and she said it's her portal. She chats away to other people on it and you can see them too. She has a new friend called Alexa who tells her things like what day it is, which at the moment is very useful!

One of the parcels was huge and Sarah panicked as she had ordered Celia a two-step, step-stool.

She was surprised at the fact it arrived within eighteen hours of ordering, but more worried that it was so enormous had she ordered the wrong thing.

It didn't even have Sarah's name on it if she had looked closely.

It was for Dave, so that was ok.

I only got out of my chair when food was in the offing.

I am enjoying people's comments about my life in isolation.

Sarah's memory is so bad that she took her camera on her last walk with Celia but forgot to put the memory card in. That speaks volumes!

Speaking of volumes, think Shakespeare, she loved this comment from her friend Mark Reid: 'Great adventures Phoebe, thanks. May I venture to suggest you may be blending your nods towards Shakespeare - with this taming of the shrew and your use of the phrase bated breath, which first appeared (as a word in the English language) in The Merchant of Venice. It apparently has nothing to do with what you may have eaten.

I'm informed it is short for abated and means to hold one's breath due to suspense, trepidation or fear. Bated; abated; lessen in amount.

Sounds like the unfortunate shrew's breath was likely 'bated.'

# 4th April

Sarah was a bit late starting to tell you all my news because,

- a: she got up late
- b: the sun was shining
- c: she said that she didn't want me to think I am the centre of the universe!

She was late getting up yesterday too!

I do worry about her; I came in at lunchtime just to see what crumbs were on offer and when she looked down realised that she was trying to slice the cheese with a potato peeler.

I had a splendid afternoon in the garden and continued to keep an eye on her just in case she did something silly and worth recording.

She did sit inside the parterre and hold a long conversation with someone called Iona. What fascinated me was I could see them both on the black box. How sweet that they waved goodbye to each other.

She said she is going to make me my very own website but is still thinking of a good name for it as Phoebe Furnackerpan is hard to spell. She wondered about www.acatsatonic.co.uk.

She has been asked to make a new page on the Unofficial Women's Institute for blogs, but she seems to have lost the message about it. Hopeless, if a moderator spots this post perhaps she could contact her again.

Celia is spring cleaning her bedroom. Sarah says she doesn't know what that means. I am sure Celia could enlighten her but she needs to make sure they both have got their hearing aids in.

It would be such a shame if the advice fell on deaf ears!

# 5TH APRIL

Sarah is funny, she makes lots of notes about things I have done during the day, then she either loses the pieces of paper or if she jots a note on her black box about it, she stares intently at the screen and goes 'Gravy, what was that all about?'

Today's offering says:

> Saturday wardrobe wheelbarrow
> Collar bling
> Gravy
> Chubby Checker
> Hearing aids
> Frogs
> Grunting

So, who was grunting?

The only grunting I heard was when Sarah decided to write yesterday's report in the garden as it was sunny.

I'm sure I heard her say, 'Now I know why the curser is called a curser.' She had great problems getting the screen in the right position to be able to see the curser, let alone use it.

She may have used some other words that I didn't expect in her vocabulary.

Chubby Checker

This is the name she has given to my friend the Tabby who spends a lot of time in our garden, a bit catty I thought, seeing as she's no lightweight herself!

At least when she says he's in the garden I don't have to get up off my cushion, in order to work out which of my friends has come to play.

Frogs

Dave and Daphne have been working in the garden and have reconstructed the old pond by the parterre. It's full of juicy frogs.

Last time I caught one in the front garden Sarah bravely took it from me and put it back in the pond. I had no idea that she was that brave. Celia 'hopped' back inside while all this was going on, and waited until it was all over.

One day I will tell you the story of the rat and her dad, Sarah's dad, not the rats.

Collar Bling

This one was easier, Daphne found a cat collar in the garden and told Celia that it was mine. Daphne isn't a cat collar specialist like Celia. I wouldn't have been seen dead in the one she found.

I don't do bling, never have, never will. I am far too sophisticated to wear such a thing, I pity the cat who wore it and admire its ability to lose it. I have lost two collars so far and they still haven't been found.

I bet the cat thought it was lost forever but what did Sarah do, she posted a photo of it on the local area Facebook page. If its owner uses Facebook it will get it back and be forced to wear it again.

Hearing aid

Celia and Sarah both have them but Sarah often forgets to put hers in which can lead to some interesting conversations when she mishears what people are saying to her. She misheard Celia yesterday but can't remember what it was about, it may have involved a wagon wheel.

That leaves us with the cryptic message 'Wardrobe and Wheelbarrow'.

Ah yes, I just remembered, Sarah went to get the wheelbarrow and said out loud to no one in particular 'Good the wardrobe is empty' as she trundled it from the front of the house around to the back where she was weeding

Last night Dave, Daphne, Celia and Sarah sat yards apart from each other to watch a film.

They can recommend the 'Green Book,' it was certainly better than the last one they watched, which I mostly slept through.

Celia then had a private viewing of 'Simon's Cat': such an enlightening cartoon that gave me lots of ideas on what to do should Celia think I need to see a vet.

Gravy Gravy? No idea what that was about!

See you all tomorrow.

Love Phoebe Furnackerpan.

# 6TH APRIL

Sarah just spent an hour writing this post and then accidentally hit the wrong button and deleted it.

What she was wittering on about was, how despite oversleeping she managed to get loads done in the garden.

Of course, she needed some supervision and I love giving advice, whether she asks for it or not.

She said she must be getting old (had she only just noticed?) as she used a kneeling stool today. She coped much better than the last time she used it. She forgot she was on it, tried to stand up to see what Celia wanted and got her legs into a sort of pretzel position and keeled over. I know beds are for lying in but not flower beds.

She did actually work quite hard (for her) and has started weeding the veg plot.

Chubby Checker romped about the garden with me again today, we played Kiss Chase and Follow the Leader.

Sarah didn't tidy her bedroom today, I thought she might but she now realises that her excuse of not having enough time to do it, isn't the real reason. She said she will tidy it when it rains, I bet she is praying for a drought.

I know she loves me a lot but I do try not to be too near her when she is washing her hands.

Have you ever heard her sing?

If you haven't you are extremely lucky. She has stopped singing 'Happy Birthday to You' and now sings 'The Owl and the Pussycat Went to Sea' when she washes her hands.

Stay safe, love Phoebe.

# 7TH APRIL

Sarah is writing this in the sun in the garden, and of course, she is sitting in the very spot I would have chosen for myself.

You really can't get the staff these days.

Today she is cremating, sorry cooking a meal, I do hope it turns out all right, she has a propensity to be a walking disaster in the kitchen.

I quickly passed through there on my way to another adventure in the garden, and she was muttering LOUDLY.

She may have been hoping for help but cooking isn't my thing.

'It's like the Great British Bake Off' I heard her shriek. 'When Stacey's oven door fell off.' I wondered why she was sitting on the floor twiddling things that she didn't even know existed in the oven. She seemed to wriggle and squirm about, head inside the oven complaining that the light never came on when you wanted it to.

More shouting rude words that should never be on a young lady's lips, but I guess we will have to overlook that as she is pretty old, she says she's had longer to learn lots of words.

Watching from my bedroom I could see she was twisting a nut that had come off and that the right side of the shelf support was flailing about. It seemed like an eternity but eventually, after much effort, she managed to get the nut in the right position.

A look of satisfaction spread over her face which was a much nicer sight than her expression a few minutes earlier.

She then turned the oven on and put nothing in it, she is strange or forgetful, probably both!

When she gives talks to the lovely ladies from the Women's Institute about being a stroke survivor, she causes a lot of laughter as she tells them about how she cooks with short term memory loss, and how she had no idea where the grape came from in the Spaghetti Bolognaise or the rubber band in the pasta.

Something smells very delicious; it is wafting out into the garden.

She is useless at multi-tasking so I think I need to nudge her to go back into the kitchen to see if anything is burning yet.

I am looking forward to telling you the outcome of her culinary exploits tomorrow.

Much love as always.

Phoebe.

# 8th April

What a day, it started very well as Sarah managed to be bribed out of bed with the offer of watching a Jane Austen film.

She sat in my favourite chair in the room they call the barn. It was a barn that was converted into a granny flat attached to their house and it's so big that everyone can socially isolate and still watch a film together (if Sarah can work the projector and laptop).

Although it was a farmhouse where they live, the nearest they get to livestock is me!

The 'gals' all enjoyed the film 'Northanger Abbey' but there weren't any cats in it so I thought it was a bit boring.

Cats are conspicuous by their absence in Jane Austen's work, with barely a mention apart from Mrs Jennings in Sense and Sensibility saying that without the Dashwood sisters' company she and Colonel Brandon will be forlorn: "…Lord! we shall sit and gape at one another as dull as two cats."

I hurt my leg last night and wouldn't let anyone touch it, but eventually, Sarah held me tightly and Celia bathed my leg and they put some powder on it.

Heaven only knows what Sarah did in the afternoon as she has no recollection of anything, other than the fact that an unexpected delivery of garden furniture arrived at threeish.

Just in time for another cup of tea and rest and to try out these new reclining chairs properly. Daphne had made some fab cookies using rosemary and chocolate, I'm not sure how

Rosemary enjoyed it or how in the lockdown she came to get to us, but I never saw her. I did see Daphne snapping off bits of a bush but I can't believe there was any connection.

Oh yes, Sarah was a bit shouty this afternoon, after a kind lady from the Unofficial Women's Institute group tried to help her put other posts onto the page. Thank goodness they only sent messages on messenger and not verbal communication. I had to put my paws over my ears and I did hear Sarah say it was a good job the profanity filter was on.

I always thought these WI women were quiet meek ladies, prone to making jam but I now realise that's not the case.

Celia kept walking past Sarah saying, 'Stop it, Sarah, just have a cup of tea and come back to it later,' but either her hearing aid battery had run out or she was ignoring her.

To cut a very long story short she got there in the end, and then came out into the garden and took lots of photos of ME and some of the flowers.

She said she is going to have an early night but I have heard that before.

## 9th April

Well for me I have had quite a relaxing day.

I haven't let on what time I came back into the house, but Celia had gone to bed and she's a night owl, Daphne is an early bird and Sarah is some form of a permanently exhausted pigeon.

Sarah says 'if people were meant to pop out of bed, they would sleep in toasters.'

She also had to ask Alexa what day it was when she finally surfaced.

I spent a lot of the day snoozing on the sofa in the sunshine.

No popping anywhere for me today!

Sarah is still having problems with her hearing, and that's after getting her hearing aids adjusted before the lockdown. I heard her ask Daphne 'Sorry I didn't catch what you said.'

'I was singing' came the reply. It was nice to hear someone happy in the garden.

There seemed to be the usual amount of grunting from Sarah as she prepared a bed to put some seeds in. I thought she was immune to her own noise but she suddenly said out loud, 'Gosh I groaned then just like my father.' Must be in her genes, talking of which, her jeans appear to have got half the garden attached to them, I would never let myself be seen like that, but she hasn't got the dexterity to lick her legs. (Although if she had dropped some ice-cream on them I think she would have a good go.)

I actually do a lot of my going out when no one is around as I don't want to make people jealous, which I think is very thoughtful of me. Sarah hasn't been outside of the garden for a whole week but did clap the NHS and blew her bugle VERY LOUDLY. It makes a change from blowing her own trumpet! I retreated inside as my ears are very sensitive and unlike her I can tell the difference between speech and singing, music and *CATerwauling*. I felt very hurt when everyone's teatime was considered of greater importance than mine.

I came into the dining room in a huff and turned my back on everyone to register my disgust.

Celia isn't usually that cruel but we all have our off days I guess.

# 10th April

What a glorious day I have had.

I decided I would like to be like Goldilocks and try out all the beds.

I sneaked upstairs without anyone knowing and found a lovely bed in the sun but Celia found me and that was that.

I then crept back and tried a bed in another bedroom, where Sarah found me.

I'm not sure which one of them is Father Bear, it's probably the grumpiest one who shall remain nameless.

Sarah has been sitting in the sun too, but not on her bed, she has been in the garden keeping her distance from everyone. This lockdown in her opinion is a bit of a trial, but she has been making the best of a bad job.

She seemed to have had the little black box firmly fixed to her ear, I reckon it might need to be surgically removed! She takes it everywhere with her, and she's not alone, everyone has got one.

She chatted away into thin air for more than an hour, I wasn't sure whether the sun had got to her, but she changed her position finding a warm shady spot while I went to sleep.

I do think the sun has affected Sarah: at one point when I was sitting on the table and peering out of the window, she grabbed me in a very unladylike way (it's a complete no-no being there) and then held me close to her and danced me around the room. How embarrassing, just supposing Chubby Checker had seen,

I would never be able to raise my tail with pride again. I thought she was going to sing to me, perish the thought, so I wriggled a bit and she put me firmly back onto the floor.

Dave and Daphne have been busy in the garden too, they were in the back garden, keeping their distance from Sarah I presume. Daphne is very organised and has been weeding around the pond and using some large pebbles made an edging between the path and the plants. I don't get it at all, I just walk anywhere I fancy. Dave removed lots of rubbish from behind the greenhouse which previous occupiers of the house had put there. Chubby Checker keeps trying to have a quick undisturbed kip in the greenhouse but the hole is now blocked where the glass is broken and Chubby has had to find somewhere else for his afternoon nap.

Speaking of Chubby, I sort of invited him into the house, well actually I think he invited himself in; he's very persuasive. Sarah, who was coming into the house to use the toilet, got the shock of her life.

Firstly, she wondered if a rat had come in, which if it had, her friend Sonia would have heard her screaming in Brussels.

She then realised it was Chubby who in a fit of conscience bolted out of the door. Sarah screamed and Celia wondered whatever had happened. I beat a swift retreat, and peered around the door when all the commotion was over just to make sure everyone was all right.

Sarah and Celia had ice-cream for pudding but none got spilt on Sarah's leg, I was disappointed, I wanted to see what her dexterity was like.

Oh yes and Chubby used my litter tray.

I laid low for the rest of the day, very low!

# 12th April

Sarah has spent most of the morning talking to disembodied voices and bodies on a new contraption that has found its way into the house. Sarah said it's a Facebook portal so she can talk to people all over the world.

I'm not sure I believe her but she did say to one cheery face, 'How are you in South Africa?'

Celia was much more considerate and included me in the conversation, picking me up and waving a paw, mine not hers, to a friend who they call Lovely Dawn.

If you could get a gold medal in the Olympics for talking, Sarah would be well on the way to a gold, Celia says she personally would get one for eating!

(Sarah nodded in agreement).

While Dave and Daphne have been working tirelessly in the garden Sarah said she felt a bit guilty, as all she had done was talking! Everyone agreed she should feel bad. (I made that up!) She definitely needs to go to Specsavers. Entering the kitchen from bright sunshine into the contrasting gloom she shouted 'Phoebe you bad cat, get down off the worktop at once!' at a black cardigan that was on the surface by the breadbin.

My eyesight is perfect, well you've never seen me wearing glasses have you?

Last week she mistook her slippers for me, this week a cardigan, it's not doing my self-esteem much good, she puts it down to the stress of not being able to go out, but I think she is either blind, or batty, or both.

I wonder what she will mistake me for next? Answers on a postcard please.

Today Daphne did an online Easter egg hunt in our garden for her grandson. She told him that she had hidden twelve Easter eggs and made a video. Poor little lad, she only showed eleven of the hiding places, I bet that kept him occupied for ages looking for the missing one!

Sarah is convulsed with laughter at the very thought, rather inappropriate in my opinion.

Celia I am sure was talking to herself in the kitchen this morning but she insists she is 'just thinking aloud.' Well it was loud enough for Daphne, Sarah and me to hear it.

I can rotate my ears 180 degrees and I have thirty-two muscles that I use to control them. I don't think either of them has got more than two. They can't even wiggle their ears, let alone use them as scanners.

I wasn't invited to see the film they were watching, a good job too, Celia spent a lot of it looking the other way.

It was 'The Aeronauts' - a gripping tale of being in a hot air balloon and going seven miles high, loosely based on a true story. Celia panics if I climb a tree, so you can imagine what she was like by the end of the film and Daphne doesn't like heights, so a jolly time was had by all!

Oh yes, and returning to the subject of Sarah needing to go to Specsavers, she fell over the picnic bench. Yes, you read it right, over the picnic bench! She went flying but not as elegantly as you would in a hot air balloon.

Spread eagled by the parterre on the gravel, she managed to get back up and will go on to fight another day.

Convulsed with laughter and wheezing like a squeezebox she has announced she is off to bed.

# 13th April

Yesterday was what everyone called Easter Sunday.

I think I might have misheard them, though I think it was 'Eater Sundae'.

Everyone had lovely things to eat but my diet remained the same, I am very grateful for what Celia gives me to eat.

I wouldn't want to complain but one of the questions that frequently comes to mind is, 'why don't the cat food companies make mouse flavour?'

Sarah thinks it's because it would be difficult to make artificial mouse flavouring. The other alternative would be having mouse farms and she says no one would want that.

Well she wouldn't that's for sure.

I must admit it wouldn't be as much fun as eating a mouse I have caught myself.

That's all part of the dining experience for me.

Anyway, I can't imagine Celia going into Tesco's and having difficulty to choose between 'Mouse Flavour', 'Dead Squirrel' or 'Unidentifiable Stinky Muck' flavour.

Well everyone's welcome to their own opinion, I think the cat food makers (she couldn't spell manufacturers) would make a killing, instead of me!

Just like me, they had lunch in the garden as it was Sunday and the sun was shining.

They didn't have the fun of pouncing upon some live food.

I don't know why but they seem to cook most things.

I can't say it appealed to me, bleugh I hate cabbage. Sometimes they eat ratatouille I wouldn't want any, they must use old rats, I never find rats are chewy.

Lots of activity in the garden today, and Sarah put on some dark glasses, I would have thought it would have made her able to see things in the dark, but as you may remember she fell over the picnic table in broad daylight, and she is still whinging about how she scraped the skin off her shin.

In the morning they sat together and listened to some singing and talked about something called Psalm 23

It was all about shepherds and stuff like that.

In the evening Sarah set up the projector and they watched something called HTB@home, which was the same stuff as the morning but the singing was much better.

I actually quite enjoyed it and sat on Celia's lap and watched intently, and I especially liked it that Nicky Gumble said if he had a cat it would be a lawyer, just like him and all his family.

At last someone appreciates a cat's intelligence.

The next film wasn't as good, so while they were busy watching it, I caught a shrew as an Easter gift, and left it dead in the kitchen for them to enjoy.

They turned up their noses and took it back into the garden.

Sometimes their ingratitude is *purrfectly* insulting.

# 14th April

I had a restful day yesterday, lying inside, in the sun.

It was a bit too cold to lie outside, Sarah wondered if I would like a cat sweater or coat.

I wouldn't be seen dead in either of those.

I don't know why people go on so much about the cold. They obviously have a design fault, why they weren't made like me, with a fur coat? I really don't understand!

Sarah says she has enough of a problem getting a hair brush through the bit of human fur on her head that she calls hair.

Below I have listed some reasons why I wouldn't wear an outfit.

1. If I wore a sweater I would be in danger of overheating.
2. I wouldn't be able to move so freely so I might have an accident.
3. It might catch on a tree branch mid-leap.
4. I would get tangled up in it (deliberately).
5. I WOULD LOOK AN IDIOT!

Lots more work was done in the garden.

I watched Sarah filling plant pots and then bury beans in them.

She really is most peculiar; I can't imagine why she has done that.

She did the same thing the other day and keeps going into the greenhouse and talking to the pots.

Is that where the expression 'potty' originated?

Have you ever heard anything so ridiculous - who does she think she is, Prince Charles?

She has just gone upstairs to get her copy of Brewer's Dictionary of Phrase and Fable, if we are lucky, she may remember what she's gone up there for!

She has returned with not one but two books, but it's not in them so she googled instead.

POTTY - adj., British. "eccentric, slightly mad, impractical.

A (usually) affectionate epithet deriving from crackpot (which itself derives from 'crack-pate'), typically used by middle-class schoolchildren in the 1950s and 1960s and is now a rather dated colloquialism."

From "The Dictionary of Contemporary Slang" by Tony Thorne (Pantheon Books, New York, 1990).

Suits her perfectly, I think.

An early night was had by all, excluding Celia, who I have previously mentioned is a night owl. I sat on her lap for a bit then sneaked upstairs.

# 24th April

Despite my bad start (according to Sarah) yesterday, I am pleased to tell you I continued in the same vein for the rest of the day, with short intermittent bursts of good behaviour. Sarah of course let the sun go to her head and never made any notes about yesterday.

The book for research came in the morning and was put six feet away from the front door because that's what you have to do with the lockdown. It was the History of SalisburyTeacher Training College.

Why, I wanted to know, was this such a source of joy?

It appears that Sarah's Grandmother and Great Aunt went there in the 1900's, and the 1910's.

She has photographs of them presumably taken at the college, in strange outfits, but I expect they would have been very surprised by what people wear these days.

The college motto 'In quietness and confidence is your strength' spoke to Sarah's heart too.

Well that's what she told me.

The ladies who wrote the book have been emailing Sarah and are being very helpful. Not just at helping her with her quest.

I overheard Sarah talking to someone about the Spanish Flu Epidemic, which was a hundred years ago, or seven hundred years in cat age.

I can't imagine why she wants to know about '*hisstory*'. I keep telling her there's no future in it!

I kept disappearing unless food was in the offing, (what is the offing?) is it another word for cat dish.

I kept a close eye on the pond as I fancied a bit of fresh fish, there's nothing like it!

People didn't seem to understand my interest in them. A lot of shooing and 'leave the fish alone' was rather a monotonous drone as I basked in the sun.

It seemed to be connected to the sunshine, if I went and snoozed in the shade of a shrub, I wouldn't hear anyone say that.

Sarah rightly pointed out that if I was asleep, I couldn't hear it, little does she know about my superpowers.

Surely, she must have observed that a rattle of my dish or the words 'here's your food,' penetrate even my deepest sleep and I am up like a shot.

I bet you didn't know that the Japanese have lots of sayings referring to cats.

As you can tell Sarah gets easily distracted, she was googling 'offing' but went off at a tangent.

What is googling? It sounds very nasty!

One Japanese saying is 'Willing to borrow a cat's paws' which translates as, 'You're willing to take help from anyone.' I'm not too sure that I am appreciated for all I do, and in Croatian, the literal translation of 'The pussy cat will come to the tiny door.' means essentially 'What goes around comes around.'

Bit like the goldfish, they just keep on coming around.

It took me ages to come through the tiny door in the old codgers back door, I didn't want to let them see how clever I am. Well not straight away, but now I have established myself as part of the family, I can afford to let my brilliance be seen.

I like it when people open the door for me instead of pushing my way through the cat flap, it's so undignified.

Some people think cats are superior, too true, I don't need to show it, I know it.

Gosh that reminds me I was challenged by Sarah to write a poem.

Hope she's forgotten, I will see if can distract her.

In Japanese the direct expression 'To wear a cat,' means to pretend to be innocent and hide one's true nature.

Do you think, 'the cat, sat on, the mat.' will do for a poem?

No, I didn't think so either, Sarah wrinkled her nose in disgust, which is never a pretty sight, she's wrinkly enough without adding to it.

Here's today's poem.

> I am as innocent as a morning rose,
> Warmed by the summer's waking sun
> I am as pure as driven snow
> When winter shows what can be done,
> I am a tempest on oceans deep
> When fury unleashes its ugly face,
> I am at home, at rest, at peace,
> Especially on Celia's knees.

Will that do?

Last night everyone got together in the barn and watched a film called 'Fisherman's Friends'.

As usual I paid great attention, but I didn't see any real fish, just nasty vicious things called lobsters.

Tomorrow I will be back in my favourite position nmmmmmmmmmmmmhhhhhhhhhhhhhhhhhhhhhhhhhhhhhhh hhhhhhhhhhhhhhhhhhhhhhhhhhhhhhhhhhhhhhhhhhhhhhhhhhhh hhhhhhhhhhhhhhhhhhhhhhhhhhhhhhhhhhhhhhhhhhhhhhhhhhhh hhhhhhhhhhhhhhhhhhhhhlkkkkkkkkkkkkkkkkkkkkkkkkkkkkk kkkkkkkkkkkkkkkkkkkkkkkkkkkkkkkkkkkkkkkkkkkkkkkkkkkk kkkbnnnnnnnnnnnnnnnnnnnnnnnnnnnnnnnnnnnnnnnnnnnnnnn nnnnnnnnnnnnnnnnnnnnnnnnnnnnnnnnnnnnnnnnnnnnnnnnnnn nnn000000000000000000… fury.

I just sneaked onto Sarah's laptop while she had nipped inside.

How amazing that the word fury came up, she will be full of fury when she finds out!

Better make myself scarce for a bit.

# 28th April

Goodness me what a cold wind again today, hardly worth going out, I might have got my fur ruffled.

Sarah felt the same, although she hasn't got any fur, just that long unruly stuff she calls hair.

Having made myself at home in the most comfortable chair in the breakfast room, I lay there half dozing and half listening in to the conversations that were going on around me.

Tomorrow Sarah is taking part in the Mass Observation Online project which involves her writing a diary of everything she does tomorrow. I have certainly given her a lot of practice!

I do hope she is as articulate as me!

Celia is going to do it too, but she will write using a pen and paper. I sometimes see Sarah scribbling on bits of paper with what she calls a biro. Mind you she then loses them and faffs about for ages trying to find them again. Sometimes if they stay lost it can be a bit stressful for all of us.

Sarah was subdued today, and felt as gloomy as the sky. She felt a bit like Winnie the Pooh on the blustery day, only not as positive. In fact, I think she was more like Eeyore, dejected and gloomy feeling, saying things like 'it could be worse, but I don't know how?'

Perhaps it's because she would like to go for a walk.

Sarah practised her culinary skills and made a delicious tea but I didn't get offered any. In fact, I sat on the window sill of the dining room and pulled faces at them and whined to be let in, but it fell on deaf ears.

They just chomped away at their pork chops, mashed potatoes and Chinese RATatouille, an experimental dish invented by Sarah, which passed the taste test. Well I didn't see anyone spit it out.

I didn't fancy fruit salad personally but it seemed a popular pudding, with everyone tucking in.

I deigned to come in at seven, for my tea.

What would cheer her up I wondered? Then I remembered it's Monday evening and there is a Zoom meeting of the East Hunsbury Literary and Nice Biscuit Society.

At eight o'clock she joined the group online to discuss their latest book, 'The Small Island,' by Andrea Levy.

As you can well imagine Sarah had started the book, struggled with her memory and then mislaid it.

Not everyone had finished it so that wasn't a problem and eased her mood slightly.

The group consisted of six local readers including Bridie who told us it seemed familiar and eventually she realised she had read it before.

Light-hearted banter ensued and once they got underway there was more of a feeling of personal interaction, rather than it being a video streaming event.

Some spoke from their bedrooms, enjoying a short while to put down all their burdens and cares and enjoy the company of likeminded bookworms.

Bridie sat in her conservatory, where John supplied her with cups of tea. Every home should have a John.

When he looked after me when everyone had gone away overnight, he came and rolled on the floor with me and enjoyed it so much he came back a second time.

Celia and Sarah were touched by this. Not literally.

Sarah seemed much happier after her time with the 'girls' but sadly no biscuits appeared, normally they have a wonderful selection. The Nice Biscuit part of the group, which to be honest was why I had come, really should be reported to the trade descriptions people. What a swizz!

Sarah went up to bed a bit earlier than usual, but Celia the night owl didn't and she had blocked my cat flap to try and keep me in.

I woke up at 4am and she had to get up to let me out. Serves her right!

# 29th April

Well, my naughty streak is still in full swing!

Some people may have thought a good night's sleep would rectify the situation.

No such luck followers, I love being naughty and pushing people's buttons.

I have pressed lots of buttons today.

Ping, there we go another one pressed.

I started the day by lying outside the bathroom door while Celia was in there.

I looked up as Sarah went to go into her special lockdown bathroom.

No-one is allowed in there and I think that might include me.

To stay on the safe side I laid down, right in front of the door.

When she came to come out, I was in exactly the spot where her right foot would go.

She wobbled a bit, hung onto the door frame and looked sternly at me but I rolled onto my back.

She always softens when I do that, and knelt down to give my tummy a good rub.

I wonder do people do that too?

Sarah went off to get dressed, brush her hair, take her tablets, and whatever else she does behind closed doors.

Celia knocked on her door and opened it saying 'Would you like a little visitor?'

I wasn't too sure that she would, but I scuttled in and was under her bed before she could say taramosalata.

I then popped out from my hiding place behind the valance and, proceeded to attack her ankles.

I soon got fed up with that, but then she may have done too, so I went downstairs to see what I could do next, Sarah says it's important during the lockdown to do things, as well as rest.

The office door had been left ajar, and there is nothing I like more than snooping around in places I'm not meant to. Sarah had a lovely red exhibition board in there, with lots of felt brooches attached to it.

Sarah had made them and put them on the board for a coffee morning, which they had before the lockdown.

Celia heard an unexpected noise and guess who it was?

You got it in one, and she came in to find I had been playing a new game called get the brooch off the board and then treat it like a mouse.

Rather unkindly in my opinion, the brooches were removed from the floor and then I was removed from the room.

I went into the breakfast room and heard a rather strange conversation.

Celia looked up from her phone and said to Sarah 'Have you got any harrowing cat stories?'

Sarah. 'Harrowing?'

Celia, 'Yes, harrowing.'

Sarah, 'Why do you want harrowing cat stories?'

Celia, 'I didn't say harrowing, I said heroine.'

Well they both have plenty of stories about me that fit the situation.

Harrowing – when Sarah removed the baby rabbit from me, and heroine, well I am sure I can think of lots of examples, I just can't think of one at the moment.

Sarah had madly said that the very next time it rained she would tidy her bedroom.

True to her word once Sarah had finished faffing about on the computer, playing on her phone, stroking me, looking out of the window, cleaning the window, listening to a podcast, researching how to make a podcast and having lunch she had run out of excuses.

Upstairs she trudged, with about as much enthusiasm as a dead dog.

Out came the black plastic sack, but I didn't spot a duster, but she says you have to take things slowly.

Very slowly, very very slowly, interspersed with cups of tea, the occasional biscuit, anything that causes distraction.

I wasn't too sure it was a good idea to take her laptop into the bedroom, it never would be.

The bedroom did look marginally better, and Sarah was better informed about the Spanish Flu Epidemic and a man on 'Who Do You Think You Are?'

# May 2020

Sarah talks to the people hiding in her black box,
they must be very small.

# 1st May

A nice man from Amazon came today. He didn't look very Amazonian, I thought he would be a very tall and graceful woman - they were in Greek mythology, but what do I know?

One of the best-known Amazon queens was Hippolyta, who was the owner of a magical girdle, given to her by the god of war Ares.

Sarah could certainly do with a magic girdle, but I'd better not say that too loudly, she is a sensitive little flower, despite her wild woman of Borneo appearance.

It must be said that when she goes and gives talks to the Women's Institutes, that she scrubs up fairly well.

Of course, in the lockdown it doesn't matter what she wears, as the only people who will see her are the people she lives with, although they have talked about having a dressing up night, a sort of Friday frock special. She wanders around in her old pair of jogging bottoms, claiming that they are her gardening clothes, but she hasn't done a lot of gardening over the last couple of days.

I must admit though the garden is looking much better since the lockdown. It looks much tidier, (no thanks to Sarah,) many thanks to Dave and Daphne, and Celia the dandelion queen.

For those of you not fully acquainted with Sarah it may come as a surprise to you that she is untidy to the nth degree.

She is a health and safety hazard on legs. This sentiment is affirmed by Celia who has the scars to show it!

Back to the man from the Amazon, the parcel that came smelt lovely, just like one of those old- fashioned hardware shops where you could get anything from a bag of compost to a fork handle.

We both had a sniff of it, I thought I could faintly get a whiff of an Amazonian mouse, but Sarah said that was unlikely as the shop would sell mouse traps, lots of them, if it was based in the countryside.

I asked Sarah if there were mice in the rainforest and she said yes, jumping mice, and rats and porcupines. I wanted to know if there were many cats there, in case I could help out.

Sarah says there are lots of cats and most of them are bigger than me, like a puma or a jaguar. I thought Puma was a make of trainers, and a Jaguar was a car. Life can be very confusing at times.

Inside the parcel was something to try and stop the Heron from eating the fish, I watched intently to see if Sarah would fall in the pond as she attempted to attach all these hexagonal plastic shapes together.

She always moans at me if I try and put my paws in the pond water, but she seemed to think it was ok for her to do it.

Sarah seemed to spend a long-time using bamboo canes to retrieve the hexagons, which had floated away from the edge of the pond, before she had clipped them all together.

It reminded her of going to the fair, with her parents in Chalkwell Park when she was small.

(She was small once.)

Anyway, there was a game where you had to hook a floating plastic duck onto a stick to claim the prize of a goldfish. She so desperately wanted one, and having won one, clutched the bag tightly all the way home.

Watching Sarah, leaning over the edge of the pond was highly amusing, bum in the air, (hers not mine) desperately reaching for floating discs.

It was enough to make a cat laugh.

I will have to remind her what's good for the goose is good for the gander, but I expect it will fall on deaf ears. If she falls in the pond will she get electrocuted by her hearing aids?

Dave came out and reconfigured the hexagons and added some bricks to stop them floating about. I do hope it works, as Sarah is very fond of the fish. She can't stand eating fish but I just love a good substantial meal of sushi.

She also did something very exciting and made my first podcast. It was a bit of a faff, and it wasn't quite right but if she has time tomorrow, she might have another go.

In the evening everyone settled down to watch a film.

It was called, 'The Greatest Showman,' I quite enjoyed it, there was lots of singing in it, fortunately, Sarah didn't remember any of the tunes so we weren't subjected to her singing, if you could call it that!

The word 'caterwauling' springs to mind, but I think that's an insult to cats.

Oh yes, I nearly forgot, I made a new acquaintance - Clarence, he lives in Bugbrooke, which made me feel a bit itchy, but he seems quite nice. He looks ok in the photos and hasn't got any bald patches where the bugs have got him so that's a point in his favour.

Sleep well comrades, I am just about to go off for a midnight snack and a stroll around the neighbourhood.

# 2ND MAY

I am sure you won't believe this but today I have been very well behaved!

I haven't found the most awkward place to lie down or get under anyone's feet.

I haven't attacked anyone's legs!

I didn't try and catch any fish or leap onto the worktop looking for a sneaky extra bit of food.

Sarah wondered if I was ill, I'm not.

Celia who thinks she is a cat whisperer couldn't fathom it out either.

It's all part of being contrary, they just never know which way I am going to jump, and I like it that way.

Keep them on their toes.

Sarah has been quite quiet too today, she has been doing sums, and we all know how much she loves that.

She has been uncharacteristically composed.

Usually, sums involve a lot of bad words, and the throwing of balls of screwed up paper, perhaps my goodness is catching.

I wonder if she is trying to keep everyone on their toes too?

It could, of course, be the calming effect of the lockdown?

Did you know that on average, cats spend two thirds of every day sleeping? That means a nine-year- old cat has been awake for only three years of its life, and they spend an average of a third of their waking hours cleaning themselves.

Not much time left for anything else then.

Sarah is sad, very sad. Not miserable, just pathetic.

She is rocking helplessly in the armchair, having just read the following joke:

*"A couple are about to go out for the evening, they are all dressed up and ready to go.*

*As they open the door to leave, the cat runs inside the house. The taxi is already outside so the woman goes to the taxi while the man goes inside to get the cat out.*

*The woman didn't want the taxi driver to know they were leaving the house empty so she told him, "My husband is on the way, he is just saying goodbye to my mother."*

*A few minutes later, the husband arrives saying, "Sorry I took so long, the stupid thing was hiding under the bed and I had to poke her with a coat hanger to get her to come out."*

Honestly, I despair, has the lockdown finally got to her?

Celia wonders what I get up to at night, could that be the reason I have been so quiet?

They will never know!

# 3RD MAY

Sarah is still worried by my continuing good behaviour, but Daphne says I have had a bit of a go at the bannisters.

Not the white ones, I'm not silly, that would really give the game away, I sneakily let out my frustration on the plain wooden one, the newel post. No need to worry needlessly then, eh Sarah?

I am glad that Sarah did some weeding yesterday, it got her out from under my feet, and meant I could choose any seat in the house to sit on. It would be easy to think that it's not worth doing a lot in the garden during the lockdown as we can't share it with any visitors, but it's very relaxing and consoling.

If Sarah is really cross and frustrated, she goes out and takes it out on the weeds which has a two-fold effect. She can let out her anger and be as destructive as she likes but at the end of it the garden looks better. I am sure there must be a lesson to learn from that. She never scratches the bannisters, which is a relief, although if she did, I could side step the blame.

If it's raining, she throws things around in her bedroom, she says it's called tidying up, but sadly, it's not as productive and satisfying as weeding. Although she does enjoy the finished result, she never seems to finish it.

A bit like painting the Forth Road Bridge, whatever that is.

Everyone handles the lockdown differently. Celia is enjoying lots of music and has the radio on when she is cooking in the kitchen. I even saw her dancing the other day, but kept quiet about it. She is playing her recorder and singing quite a lot too.

Dave has enjoyed slowing down but is hoping for some work this week. He's a plasterer and decorator but has managed to get some work in properties that are empty at the moment. He's a chilled-out sort of guy but was a bit concerned that his hair was getting a bit long.

Daphne has been doing some work from home, planning for when she goes back. She and Dave have worked miracles in the garden. Daphne is a very keen reader and some of the time she will be seen relaxing with a book. Hairdressing isn't something we've seen Daphne doing before, but I enjoyed watching her give Dave a quick trim in the garden.

Sarah is, of course, enjoying taking down my dictation, which takes a fair chunk of the day, she is very slow.

She is enjoying watching things on her laptop and phone. She can get very distracted, but I soon remind her of what she is supposed to be doing. When I am asleep or exploring, I have no idea what she does, but she seems to be managing to keep herself occupied.

She said she might do some embroidery this week, or some painting and watch more of the sign language course.

When the daily announcements about Corona Virus are given Sarah gets very distracted, watching the person who is doing sign language, and can only recognise the occasional word.

Mind you it doesn't take much to divert Sarah's attention, I can disturb her train of thought very easily.

That's probably one of her biggest problems, short term memory, the lack of it!

She has just come upstairs into her bedroom to replace a hearing aid battery, and I watched her as she put the new battery in and then proceeded to try and put both hearing aids into one ear.

They didn't fit!

At that stage, I thought it best to remove myself from her bedroom, before she did anything else.

Then she went to take the SD card out of the camera but removed the battery. That would be why it didn't work.

Tomorrow may be book club on Zoom and has she read the book? Well, what do you think!

# 4TH MAY

Is this the lull before the storm?

The third day of impeccable behaviour, possibly because I have been asleep a lot during the day and doing things at night when no one can see what I am up to.

I spent the morning pretending to be asleep, I do a very good impression. Unlike Sarah, who to her shame has been known to drop off to sleep whilst in a group of people and has woken herself up snoring.

As her father so often said, 'You can only take Sarah somewhere twice, the second time to apologise!'

Sarah says she often said the same thing about him.

They must have been a formidable duo.

I might have dozed a little, in the morning when they all got together but they didn't sing or anything which was a great relief as I have very sensitive hearing.

After lunch together, everyone went off to do something useful. Sarah went to bed, she had planned to watch something on YouTube in her bedroom, I bet you can guess what happened next.

Talk about a deep sleep, she slept through Celia bawling that dinner was ready and she slept through the bell that Celia rang furiously to let her know.

If I had been around, I would have jumped on her, but I had already had a sleep on her bed earlier in the day and didn't want to outstay my welcome.

Eventually bleary-eyed and tousle-headed (mind you her hair is nearly always like that.) shc staggered into the room and took her seat.

After wailing to be let into the lounge with everyone else, I then settled down on the settee and proceeded to sleep through the programme they were watching.

Everyone said how good it was, the programme (not my sleeping,) and that they had really enjoyed it, and found it inspiring.

Following Sarah's earlier example, I had gone into a deep sleep and was chasing mice in my dreams, my paws were twitching and every now and then my body would jump. That was when I caught the mice. I must admit my gifts were much better received in the land of nod, than when I leave them in real life, by my food bowl.

Celia played her recorder in her bedroom, she's quite good and I could tell what she was playing, unlike Sarah's singing which I know I have mentioned before.

Due to her memory loss, she often can only remember the first line of a song and if I hear her sing 'Standing on this Mountain Top' one more time and never getting off the mountain top, I will, I will, oh I don't know what I will do, but I wish they made earplugs for cats.

I wonder if her singing is so bad because she is deaf, as she can't hear how dreadful it is.

Perhaps if she put her hearing aids in when she sings, she might shut up.

I may have told you this before, I asked her once if she was tone-deaf, but she replied that no she wasn't, she told me she is tone dumb, which means she can hear it's out of tune but can't do anything to correct it.

Well, that's a shame, not just for me, I hasten to add.

She's quite a good dancer, but very shy about it, I think it would be preferable to serenading us.

Mmmm, I may have said enough, at least you have a true picture of the torture I have to endure.

Think I need to shut my trap (my mouse trap!!!) and let you go and do something else.

I am still laughing at my own joke. Sarah says that's very bad and you should never laugh at your own jokes.

I do worry about her.

Now that no one is around I can get up to what I like, so on that note I will love you and leave you.

Until tomorrow.

Phoebe

# 5TH MAY

'What is the matter with Phoebe?'

This is the question on the tip of everyone's tongues.

That and, where can you get flour, eggs, and toilet rolls?

As I sleep most of the day, Sarah suspects I must be ultra-busy at night, although you might wonder looking at Sarah's face today if she is too.

We both look a little worn out.

Sarah has been having vivid dreams along with half the population during lockdown. 3D, technicolour with around sound audio.

There seems a lot of anxiety in our dreams, I dream that Celia has gone away and I'm left at the mercy of Sarah, who can't be trusted to remember to feed the fish, let alone a cat.

Celia dreams that there is a short supply of suggestive biscuits.

Dave can't get to sleep because the sugar in the butterscotch Angel Delight has overstimulated his brain, so no dreams there. Sarah thought Daphne was taking a big risk letting him lick out the bowl!

Daphne probably dreams that slugs are attacking her vegetable seedlings in the greenhouse.

Sarah read that our dreams work to help us handle difficult emotions we might not have been able to process during the day.

She had shocking nightmares the other night.

We may be dreaming vividly about things we might be missing in the lockdown. This helps us process grieving, yearning, and loss.

Is Sarah missing toilets in the lockdown? I don't think so, as she has got her own isolation bathroom and no one else is allowed in there, so it's always available. However, a lot of her dreams revolve around toilets or the lack of them. One night she spent the whole dream searching for toilets only to find they all were the gents. What was she doing by Southend Pier, rushing up the High Street, dashing into shops that had no toilets, she even tried the Registrar's Office at the Civic Centre in Victoria Avenue.

Finally, she woke up and went like a bat out of hell to her bathroom.

Lots of people are sleep deprived a lot of the time, (that doesn't include me of course) and they are catching up with sleep - and waking up without an alarm makes remembering their dreams more likely.

I wonder if Celia twitches in her sleep, I will have to creep up on her in the night or early hours in the morning and have a good look.

I have mooched about the garden quite a bit, inspecting the weeding, some people are better than others. I will mention no names but the Dandelion Queen seemed a little slack at the moment. I am sure she is so busy that it slips her mind. She spends a lot of time on the phone, catching up with people. Celia has now has been demoted and is now Dandelion Princess and Daphne has taken up her mantle.

Sarah has had some splendid video conversations with old friends. Some of them were very old, but I won't divulge their names. I think Brussel sprouts might have been mentioned by one of them, but I could be mistaken, and I've been told it's rude to hang around just listening, hoping for a piece of juicy gossip.

Oh well, another day in lockdown has been survived.

I wonder what people will dream about tonight?

# 7TH MAY

I have kept a fairly low profile today.

That means laying down anywhere, but especially where people can fall over me.

This afternoon in the garden I kept throwing myself at Sarah's feet, some may ask if I was overcome with cheesy smells, but that wasn't the case.

If there was a spot of concentrated sunshine, I would lay down on my back seductively to entice Sarah to stroke my tummy.

It worked the first couple of times, but Sarah is a fickle creature and seemed keener to talk to her plants in the greenhouse. I can't see the appeal, after all they aren't going to respond by draping themselves over her, lavishing love and affection, and mouse breath.

Mind you I don't do that too often either.

No sign of Chubby Checker for a few days now, someone suggested that perhaps I was withdrawn because I was pining for him, or a boyfriend in general.

Celia wondered if my behaviour of late is hormonal, as Sarah suggested that perhaps I had gone through my kitten phase. That of course means I am entering my adolescent, teenage years, which involve sulking when I don't get my own way, and being stroppy.

Am I turning into 'Kevin the Teenager,'? Has my quietness been misjudged as tiredness and instability, instead of the usual teenage qualities of inability to get out of bed and rational thought?

Are Celia and Sarah reverting to their teenage selves as they don't like getting up in the morning, and stagger downstairs, dishevelled and moody.

Celia says I should point it out to you, that she doesn't appear dishevelled and moody, that's Sarah's lack of dress sense, with rational thought sadly lacking.

Celia arrives late, but always looks neat and tidy around the edges. She says 'Sorry,' a thousand times and gets her suggestive biscuits and eats them for breakfast, even though it's actually, time for elevenses, or possibly twelvesies.

By this time, I have already had my breakfast, lovingly prepared by Celia, who having dished it out at the crack of dawn, goes back to bed for a further snooze.

Dave and Daphne are up with the larks and bustling about while snoozing continues upstairs.

Now that I am a teenager, I feel entitled to be sulky, and mooch about, going out late, returning in the early hours of the morning.

Emotionally the lockdown is taking its toll.

Sarah keeps on about a black dog, I can't imagine why, I would have thought a black cat like me would be enough.

She says some people find this black dog following them around, and it's not a nice gentle miniature poodle called Liquorice or a bouncy black Labrador named Guinness.

It's more like a Rottweiler, looking large and menacing, (I do think they don't get a good press, some of them are very nice. Mind you I wouldn't want to be down an alley with one on a dark night.)

Sarah says she has a black dog that threatens her sometimes. I am surprised because the only dog I have seen her with is a white one called Hugo, that Celia bought her for her last birthday and sometimes sits on her bed.

She thinks it's very important to keep in touch with people during the lockdown and yaps away on her phone, to all and sundry.

Lots of people, according to her, are finding life difficult at the moment. They feel isolated, or worried, a bit scared or helpless, but that's perfectly normal.

She is trying to focus on the things she can control, (which obviously excludes me), like who she talks to and not listening too much to the radio reports.

Once a day is enough to listen to updates, too much information can drag her down and then she finds the black dog prowling around.

Sadly, she hasn't got such good control over what she eats, but you can't be good at everything. I think I heard her saying she would like some chocolate but her Easter eggs are finished. She asked Daphne, who is going shopping tonight, for a bag of sugar free Werthers.

I wonder if her black dog has got a name?

Sarah likes unusual names so it would probably be called Arbuthnot, or Montmorency Augustus Crump; it certainly wouldn't be called Fluffy because that's a cat's name, or Sprinkles Honeydew Bluff which makes it sound a friendly dog, which it is not.

I think the time is drawing near when I will go off for my nightly perambulation around the neighbourhood.

Sarah did say some people look forward to hearing about me and it cheers them up. She would say 'I can't imagine why anyone would be cheered up by a VERY naughty cat!' but I can imagine why, it's because I am so adorable.

I will finish with an interesting cat fact.

The two oldest cats on record lived to thirty eight and thirty four years old. Both were owned by the same owner and lived on a diet of bacon, eggs, broccoli and coffee.

I do hope Celia reads this I've never tried any of those things.

Correction, I have tried broccoli, when a bit fell on the floor. It was bleurgh, yuk, double yuk, horrible.

Have a lovely day one and all.

## 8TH MAY

Friends, Romans, countrymen, lend me your ears!

I can feel a spate if naughtiness creeping up on me.

Sarah came down to breakfast to find me standing on the table, I grinned then laid down.

Sarah did not grin (well actually I think she was trying to conceal her humour, badly!) and told me to get down.

I think she is happier now that I have a bit of mischief in me.

Actually, it was a sad day in some ways, it started when Sarah went to sit in the garden to write and she spotted Augustus the goldfish floating on the top of the water.

Fearing the worst, she went over to see if he was breathing. He wasn't. She considered giving him the kiss of life, but was worried she might overdo it and that he would blow up like a balloon.

Anyway, she doesn't like the taste of fish.

Celia and Daphne came and sat at the table where Sarah was clacking away, guess what they were having for lunch?

Mackerel – 'mmm, yummy fish' said Daphne.

I thought it might touch a raw nerve in Sarah, but she stoically carried on eating her lunch with a slight wrinkle of her nose at the thought of eating Augustus.

He had a full ceremonial burial in the garden, Sarah wishes she had played the last post on her bugle but she's not that good.

When it's the 8pm clap for the NHS the neighbours say she is improving, but I think they are really just being kind.

I don't know where Augustus was put but I will see if I can find him. Sarah has marked the spot but I don't know what with.

This afternoon Sarah rewrote the final story for her next book. She seems to like it more than the first draft so that is encouraging, I am hoping she will do more gardening and things, and less clacking.

She did do some weeding in the front garden but it was accompanied by her groaning loudly every time she tried to get up, along with audible complaints about her right knee.

I don't know who Arthur Itus is, but she does moan about him, although I have never managed to see him.

When she was small, she had an imaginary friend called Peter and she insisted that he had a place laid at the table for him. Her mother obliged but I do wonder if it was just a ruse to get some extra food.

Thinking about it, Sarah was an atrociously picky eater and meal times were a battle of wills.

I expect she wanted Peter there as back up.

As you well know, she outgrew that stage and doesn't struggle with food at all, except for fish which I have already mentioned. In fact, the tables are turned and it's dieting that is her battle ground.

I do wonder if she has thrown in the towel and lost that fight during the lockdown. I notice that she does make a few attempts to curb things, but they are usually foiled when she returns from gardening and thinks she needs a little sustenance. (biscuits spring to mind!)

Celia wondered if Sarah's giddy spell was anything to do with needing sugar.

Sarah quickly used the opportunity to have a slice of bread and chocolate spread. It didn't do anything, until she went to bed and then she got raging indigestion.

Serves her right!

# 10TH MAY

Sarah seems to have got a bit muddled about what she put up when, so this is an extra entry today to hopefully bring everything up to date!

Guess who forgot to take notes yesterday?

Guess who thinks she has lost a day completely somewhere?

I am sure your guess will be as good as mine, it begins with S.

I think the sun must have gone to her head, it was so glorious and she clacked away on the laptop like nobody's business.

I wonder if brilliant sunshine makes you work faster, it was certainly mood lifting.

I tiptoed around the edge of the pond in the afternoon.

Gosh I nearly forgot to give you this awful piece of news.

I was nearly usurped by another cat, who did my job in the garden. The heron has made another appearance, early in the morning before some people were up.

Daphne heard a noise and looked out and couldn't see anything unusual. The noise happened a second time, so she looked out of the bedroom window and there in the garden was a very handsome tabby cat with a white bib.

She hadn't seen him before. She then looked to see what he was eyeballing, he was staring out a heron which was on the small barn roof, eyeing up its breakfast.

The combination of the cat and Daphne spooked the heron and it flew off.

Dave said I had better watch my step or my place might be taken.

I don't think so.

Anyway, Sarah put a message on our local Facebook East Hunsbury page to say 'We would like to express our thanks to the tabby cat with the white front who bravely stared out the heron who was eyeing up our pond.'

One of the replies was this. 'Miss Phoebe was holding court further along Barn Owl last evening, flirting with another of 'The Boys', Billy Cat'.

This was the same person who commented that Sarah had been let out yesterday and then she told everyone that I had been going into Billy's house, using his cat flap. She is a very sharp-eyed neighbour, so I had better watch my step.

What surprised Sarah was my reluctance to use my own cat flap and yet I had the temerity to use Billy's.

Eventually a very nice man put up an 'identicat' photo of his cat who is extremely handsome.

The mystery was solved, I must make his acquaintance, the cat not the man.

We have offered the cat a reward, we were going to give him a bag of treats, but realise if he comes again, he might find it difficult to carry the bag back home, although he looks so capable, he might be able to.

Celia is reading a book, I do hope she is enjoying it, I keep hearing her say things like 'Oh, no,' 'Gosh,' and 'How awful.' It was nice to see her reading and relaxing in the garden, in the sun, in her hat.

A film was watched, in the evening, but it didn't sound my cup of tea, so I didn't bother to join them.

Now if they said they were going to put a good cat film on I would be there like a shot.

I'm not too keen on 'The Sound of Mews Sick' it just doesn't appeal; musicals aren't my thing and *'Kitty Kitty Bang Bang'* sounds as though someone is going to shoot a cat.

I think *'The Clawshank Redemption'* might be ok, but *'Prince of Purrsia'* sounds my sort of film a bit more, regal and refined.

All I can hear is this song going through my head is 'Doh, ray, *meow'*

Better get out of here before anyone starts singing.

Especially Sarah.

# 12TH MAY

Sarah said she doesn't feel like doing anything today other than hibernating with a good book or a film.

She wasn't that active yesterday either, but then neither was I.

If she could go out for a walk she would, but unfortunately, she can't, so she will just have to make the most of walking around the garden, but it's so cold and windy it's not that appealing.

I am curled up in the armchair near where Sarah is writing, I must admit I don't blame her, I haven't ventured out either.

Yesterday was a quiet day, the peak of excitement was watching Boris read his statement which was a bit hard to follow.

I can go out anywhere I like, at any time I like, even though Celia tried to get me to stay in last night.

I did not comply with her wishes, which is a posh way of saying I will do what I want, when I want, where I want!

Dogs are very different, they aim to please their owner, such a thought never enters my head.

Well there are the odd exceptions like being nice to Celia before I get fed.

I know dogs are good at fetching things, like slippers and newspapers, but they are high maintenance and need lots of toys and things to chew on to keep in practice and they all cost money. Me, I am happiest with an empty box and they don't cost anything.

The nice man from Amazon gives us very nice quality boxes when he comes.

Dogs need to be amused a lot of the time, whereas I am a great napping companion. I can sleep all day with hardly a movement of a whisker, like I did the day Sarah thought I had chosen her bed to die on!

I don't need to be taken on walks. I have a suspicion that Celia has got a cat harness hidden away should I ever need to escort her on a walk, but I can assure you *CATegorically* that I will refuse to wear it. I wouldn't be seen dead in a red one, it's bad enough wearing a luminous green collar. Dogs on the other paw have leads and collars: pooch apparel, is popular with some owners. Can you imagine a cat wearing canvas baseball shoes, or a cute striped vest, or a waterproof doggy coat? Get a life, we are far too aristocratic and aloof to even contemplate such a thing.

The only good thing is that dogs have a lead, which I guess they use to drag their owners to places they wouldn't have otherwise visited, like lampposts and into bushes.

Last night everyone gathered around the whirring box and huge pictures of people and things appeared, on a screen in the lounge.

I know why it's called that, because it's where I lounge and loll about. Sarah's bedroom could be called the same, but it would get a bit confusing.

Dogs would be afraid and cower behind the settee and probably throw up there too, at the sight of Boris, larger than life on the screen. I was expecting him to be ferocious, but he was quite docile, I nonchalantly watched from a distance and reserved my judgement, inscrutable is my middle name!

When it was bedtime, I had no intention of climbing in my basket and dozing even though Celia tried to get me to stay in. So off I went to wander the streets, meet up with my nocturnal buddies and explore the neighbourhood.

Adios Amigos!

Sleep well, stay safe.

# 14TH MAY

I have had a wakeup call.

At 5am I slunk into Celia's room and watched the rise and fall of her body as she slept. She looked very peaceful, but her sleep was about to be disturbed by me as I wanted to go out. If she blocks my cat flap at night she has to take the consequences!

Rude awakening on the cards for Celia.

I try not to be too rude, just gently climb on her bed, then scoot across it until I am aligned with her spine and then walk up it until I get to her head, then head butting her until she responds.

Having got a drowsy response, I meow until she is prepared to get out of bed. Shuffling out of her bedroom into the hall she half -heartedly shrugs her shoulders, slowly goes down the stairs, and shuffles the rest of the way to my bedroom. She removes the obstruction in front of my exit and makes the return journey to her room.

Now if that had been Sarah it would have been a different scenario altogether.

She wouldn't have tried to keep me in, giving her no reason to make a nocturnal expedition to the far-flung corner of the house.

I have tried waking her up. Aware of something walking over her in bed, she would either shoo me away firmly, or would have given me a quick stroke and turned over. I like to think she is faintly comforted by my presence, but not emotionally blackmailed to do anything for me.

Off I pop into the garden, and watch the day unfold.

Sarah thinks I might be in a bit of a romantic frame of mind, by my choice of words this morning, but I can assure you after Chubby Checker pooped in our garden yesterday, I have gone off him temporarily.

I had a lovely time with Sarah in the garden this afternoon. I think she said she was weeding in the flower beds, well, I hope that's what she said!

We had a great game of hide and seek and she kept putting her hand under the box hedging and then I tried to catch it. We were quite evenly matched, the element of surprise was there and it was a battle to see whose reactions were the fastest. I will let you guess the outcome.

The wind thrashed around us and whipped me into a frenzy of activity.

I looked balletic as I twirled and spun around, moving with grace and flicking my tail with precision.

Needless to say, Sarah did not look like a Darcy Bussell pirouetting, or Margot Fonteyn (who she calls Maggot Fountain) as I led her a dance around the garden.

The word elephantine would be a better description as she pranced about trying to take photos of me showing my athleticism and poise.

I expect she will show me the results, of the photography, not her dancing - which would probably be a peek at the bruises she got as the tripped the light fantastic.

In the evening I sat in the lounge watching them eat, and they then decided to watch a film that comes out of the whirring machine. Sarah told me it is called a projector, and massive people suddenly appeared on the screen opposite where I was sitting. That was enough for me, I couldn't tolerate another evening of them engrossed in something other than me, so I went off and explored in the garden until it was dark.

Well, that's where I let them think I go, but little do they know that I go to Billy Cat's house sometimes, where I get a warm welcome as long as I don't touch his food.

I wonder if Celia will barricade my cat flap again or will she have learnt her lesson?

Only, time will tell, well that's not exactly true, I've never heard time speak so it may be up to me spill the beans.

Sweet dreams my friends.

# 16TH MAY

What an enjoyable day we have had.

Sarah ventured out into the garden and did some more weeding.

I really don't get it. She pulls out what looks a lovely plant or some luscious grass from the flower bed and then says she is going to put new plants in. Why?

Why can't she just leave it as it is, surely that would make far less work? In fact, she wouldn't have to do any work at all, that way she would have more time to play with me.

I was in a playful mood and as well as leaping around the garden, chasing my tail, playing hide and seek, and entertaining feline visitors, it seemed as if every time Sarah needed to go upstairs, I was there too. I was more than willing to trip her up or reach out through the bannisters to pat her.

Yuk she was in a very daring mood and said 'Shall I give you a kiss?' She's probably got one of those 'kiss me quick' hats that were so popular at Southend.

After all she is an Essex girl.

To keep her on her toes (I do love the element of surprise) when she bent over to kiss my head, she seemed quite befuddled when I didn't back off.

I thought it was hilarious! I hadn't laughed so much for at least ten minutes.

She went into the greenhouse again, it's not green, why are things connected to gardening such a conundrum? Chat, chat, chat she went to her seedlings.

They're not great conversationalists, now, if she said that she was growing catnip that would be a different story and I might take a bit more interest.

Talking of which Daphne came in and said to Celia, 'have you seen what Phoebe has just brought in?' Celia flinched, as it probably needed disposing of, whatever it was.

Reluctantly Celia made her way to my bedroom and there on the floor was a mouse. Not an ordinary mouse either, it had a tattoo, No, kidding, on its side it said 'King Catnip.' Celia laughed at it, which I thought was a bit unkind and brought it in to Sarah who is a musophobiac (someone with a fear of mice and rats - I do like learning new words.) If it been a live mouse or even worse a wild rat you would have heard her screaming in Kathmandu.

That sounds a lovely place to be, providing Sarah wasn't screeching her lungs out. It sounds so mystical and magical but best of all it starts with Kat. It certainly sounds a bit more interesting than Catford or Catterick which sounds like someone coughing up a hairball.

Sarah says it's very easy to get side-tracked when looking on Google, (whatever that is) and find yourself looking at funny British place names and chortling over the thought of living at Fudgepack upon Humber, or Jolly's Bottom in Cornwall. She's easily amused.

Oh, I nearly forgot to tell you I was photographed sunbathing on the roof of a neighbour's shed. Well she lives the other end of the Close, which reminded me of Julie Walters in the shoe shop sketch saying 'well he's not my husband, but he rubbed up against me in a sport jacket, which is as good as.'

I certainly annoyed Chip the dog who lived there!

My photograph was then distributed on a forum!

Talk about letting the cat out of the bag, is nothing sacred but it was a lovely way to start the day.

When I felt ignored at teatime in the lounge, I decided to let my annoyance be known and went to scratch the white paint off the door.

A chorus of 'No Phoebe, stop it at once!' forced me to find myself somewhere else to spend the rest of the evening.

Oh yes, Sarah has taken a photo of the '*purr*'loined mouse so if any cats are reading this and recognise it as theirs, we will return it.

# 17TH MAY

Well it's a good job that I haven't got a phobia of mice and rats, as Daphne and Dave saw a cat in our garden making off from behind the Japonica bush with something larger that a mouse.

It was the same gallant hero who stared the heron out. They did debate whether to tell Sarah, but they did and she is now a bit twitchy about going outside.

As she is shielding (from what I ask myself?) it's important that she spends sometime getting fresh air and benefits from the sunshine.

I have noticed that when it's cloudy, she seems a bit grumpier, in which case I need shielding from her.

We did spend some time together in the garden today, which was pleasant.

Celia went out shopping and got lost. She had gone to the Tesco Express which is about a mile from home and lost her bearings.

Thankfully she found her way back or I would have been very hungry, I'm not sure I can trust Sarah to remember to feed me.

Daphne went shopping in the morning and brought me some treats, which was very unexpected. She came back with lots of bags which were unpacked in the kitchen and swiftly put away. Daphne is our designated shopper, which is very kind of her. She gallantly queues outside the supermarkets keeping her distance from the other shoppers.

Some days are just quieter than others, today was one of those days. I mooched around the garden and further afield. I think Celia will never know what I have been up to but Sarah seems to have friends everywhere who keep blowing my cover.

I still can't get over how well known I am.

I expect you have realised I am a great Shakespeare fan, either that or my education was fairly stunted in terms of reading.

Sarah thinks that when she was at school it used to be that Shakespeare was compulsory reading as well as classics like Charlotte Bronte's 'Jane Eyre' and Charles Dickens, with a bit of George Orwell thrown in.

I wonder what children read in school these days?

Maya Angelou, Carol Ann Duffy and Seamus Heaney I expect, but I hope they get a bit of Shakespeare too.

The point of telling you this is to strengthen the importance of my next quotation. Joaquin Miller.

'Fame lulls the fever of the soul and makes Us feel that we have grasped an immortality.'

Sarah says I need to go to sleep as I seem a bit overtired today, but that's quite normal for me as I am a night stalker in the neighbourhood.

So, as you sleep, remember I am on the loose, well until I get fed up, then I will come back home, because home is where my heart is, and it's where I get fed!

# 19th May

Some days are memorable and some are not. I think today falls into the latter category, mostly because I spent most of it sleeping!

I had my breakfast at about ten and then snoozed in the lounge until everyone came bundling in and making themselves at home. Well, I suppose it is our home so I mustn't complain too much. I think they have the attitude that it's their home and they are very charitable to allow me into their inner circle. I'm not sure I agree with that, but I try to make the best of a bad job.

Once in the lounge they put on some music which although very calming to them, didn't do much for me.

I couldn't sit through that and then them all reading aloud. I know when I am beaten, so I retreated to doze on Celia's bed, who later on made the statement that it was the first time I had slept on her bed for any length of time.

She, of course, doesn't know what I do when she is out, but with the lockdown, secrets are hard to keep, as we all are under each other's feet during the day.

Fortunately, no one has got really big feet, so that's a mercy.

Normally on a Sunday, their main meal would be at lunchtime, but times are different and that includes mealtimes. While I was whiling away the hours, dreaming of carloads of mice being dropped off in the back garden, (meals on wheels!) and me dancing in the treetops, I just left them to get on with whatever they wanted to do.

Early in the evening, the doorbell rang and it was Amanda, the nice lady, but I do wonder if she is a spy. Not only had she managed to take a photo of me sunning myself on the roof of her shed, but she now came returning my collar that I thought I have been so clever to lose.

Dave expressed his gratitude and returned to the dining room where Celia was very impressed that it had made its way back.

As I said, it didn't come under its own steam. Just in case you got the wrong idea. Sarah says a homing device for collars could make a lot of money, but she is too busy taking down my dictation to find the time to invent one.

I decided that after lying on Celia's bed for six hours it was time for me to make my presence known again.

After a snack, I wandered back to the lounge where everyone had gathered again to watch something on the screen. Usually it bores me, but Celia has noted that when they all watch Holy Trinity Brompton Church that I sit with them quietly and look at it too.

Well, that wasn't quite true because, on the pretence of sitting on Sarah's lap, which I rarely do, I crept forward to have a play on the laptop keyboard. Needless to say, Sarah grabbed me and held me very tight. Celia firmly said, 'Sarah put her down, she's not happy.'

Looking puzzled Sarah grimaced and mouthed 'how do you know?' 'It's her tail, I can tell she's not happy.'

Once safely back on Celia's lap, I waved my tail defiantly just to make the point clear.

It was dark outside when everyone began thinking about going to bed, but for me, the night was yet young.

To finish off here's tonight's interesting cat fact.

Cats have some of the most unique eyes in the animal world: Instead of having circular pupils like humans, the black parts in the centres of their eyes are vertical - which can adapt quickly and can open and close like the aperture of a camera.

Sarah knows lots about cameras, and hers seems to be constantly attached to her, at least I am a beautiful subject for her to photograph my every movement.

# 21st May

What a glorious day it is in the garden, sun shining, birds singing, and Sarah is ready and waiting for me, to take down my dictation.

I think the heat may have got to Sarah as she grabbed the hoover and whizzed around downstairs with it. I do hate the hoover, it's such an aggressive machine and the noise, oh the noise, in such close proximity.

I saw Daphne speed off on her bike this morning, she has got a part-time voluntary job during lockdown. It's at a bakery so I do hope she doesn't loaf about! That would be very unlikely as she's a focused sort of person.

I could imagine if Sarah worked in a bakery or a deli, she would greet the customers with 'Your order's bready!' I expect the customer would reply, 'It's the yeast you could do!'

Has the sun gone to Sarah's head?

Once again, send your answers on a postcard please.

Celia went out too today. It was her first visit to a big supermarket and she was slightly nervous. Used to ambling around the supermarket and going wherever she wanted, at her own pace, the thought of all the markings on the floor and the restrictions were a bit daunting. She returned home victorious, carrier bags full of things that she had on her list.

The most important thing on her shopping list was of course my food. She didn't confess until she got back home that she only had one day's worth of sachets left. Good job I didn't know as I might have got a bit anxious. At least she is more reliable than Sarah, I don't know whether I would trust her to get my meals, but she has *Categorically* told me that she has done that task lots of times.

The next most important thing was Werther's sugar-free sweets, for Sarah not me, and it took poor Celia ages to find them. Sarah would have homed in on them like a magnet drawn to steel.

I hung around Celia for my next meal, but she was in no rush to feed me and an hour and a half later she decided to get around to it.

Not that I'm complaining or anything (Sarah says, 'look me in the eye and say it again,')

I wouldn't, but to display my feelings about the delay I went off and was equally slow to return. That always worries Celia.

In fact, I went off after supper at eight o'clock and didn't return until eleven the next morning. I do hope Celia managed to sleep, Sarah was totally oblivious, but that's nothing new.

I don't know what they did last night and I don't think Sarah can remember either.

# 23RD MAY

Brilliant sunshine greeted me this morning when I finally woke up.

I think I might be catching some of Sarah and Celia's bad habits!

Sarah was straight outside with her breakfast and said it reminded her of being on a cruise.

You might be surprised to know, well I was, that Sarah is well-travelled.

Her father worked for the P&O for many years and cruises were a very cheap holiday for staff as the company wanted the boat to be as full as possible.

Her mother Betty said she didn't want to go, but after much persuasion she gave in. She was shy like Sarah and couldn't face anything that took her out of her comfort zone.

I know all about comfort zones! I have my special places: Sarah's bed when she forgets to shut her bedroom door, or always the seat someone wants to sit on. I think they do that so the seat is warm when they sit on it, the height of laziness in my opinion. I sometimes sleep on the flowerbed and that makes Sarah really mad when she has just planted seedlings. It's a bed for goodness sake, and they are made for lying in.

Sarah has just got distracted and googled, why are flower beds called beds? Alexa doesn't know either. And neither does Brewers Dictionary of Phrase and Fable.

This will now become a mission to find out why.

Apart from sitting sunning herself while she pretended to look industrious, she did trim a hedge, read a bit of her new book that she had got from Amazon (for research purposes,) and cooked the evening meal and tackled a job she hates doing. In the kitchen is a plumbed in water heater so boiling water is always on tap.

Unfortunately, Celia pointed out that it had a flashing light which meant it was furred up.

You can imagine what I expected it to look like on the inside! Would it be tabby, tortoiseshell, ginger, or black like me? It wasn't anything like that at all. It had flaky bits of stuff in it, which Sarah had to get out and used descaler to clean it.

She had to stand on some steps to get the lid off and then unscrew the screws. She did a lot of huffing and puffing, she does that particularly when she has to do something that she doesn't want to.

It was a right rigmarole, emptying it, descaling it then filling it up and draining it and filling it up and draining it and filling – you get the picture; I don't feel I need to keep repeating myself.

A nice man from Hermes came today with a huge parcel. Why do these courier firms use the names of Greek gods?

Hermes means messenger, perhaps if he calls again, he could teach Sarah a bit more on how to tell what I am trying to communicate.

The parcel was for Celia and it was a shopping trolley, not any old trolley but in Sarah's Words, 'The Rolls Royce of shopping Trolleys.'

It has six wheels, overkill in my view. what do I know about trolleys, other than I could be taken out for a ride in it, but that would really damage my street cred?

The wheels are shock-absorbing, and it has brakes on it.

Rolls Royce or no Rolls Royce, I wouldn't be seen dead in one. It was a bargain, and very sturdy.

Sarah cooked the meal last night, and didn't set off the smoke alarms, so things must be on the up!

I felt a bit peckish and tried to cajole Celia into giving me an extra sachet of my special food.

She stood her ground and said I had a whole bowl of biscuits that I could eat if I was hungry.

I thought that was very nasty and so I was very naughty, to see if I could get her to change her mind. Like the shopping trolley she was very sturdy, resisting my advances, and trying to ignore me.

I leaped onto the Welsh dresser and started chewing pieces of paper and just as I was about to start on a box Sarah swept me up, and danced me around the room.

How humiliating, after that I decided to go out, I didn't want to risk another mortifying outburst, especially as Sarah might start singing.

At midnight Sarah was still doing the wretched boiler, but it was working properly by the time she went to bed.

# 24th May

Cats get skittish - dancing, and prancing about, like ballerinas on acid, when the wind is blowing. Well this one does! Pirouetting is a dangerous thing to do at any time, but when a gale is blowing it's much riskier.

Feeling frisky I twirled and leapt, sometimes all four feet were in the air at the same time. I felt quite proud of my agility and bravado. Did someone say pride comes before a fall?

Surely not.

I had spent a lot of the morning dozing, inside the sun was shining, but the wind was vicious and I felt like spending the morning relaxing.

Daphne and Dave on the other hand were up drinking tea at five o'clock following the smoke detector going off, which woke everyone. Thankfully it was a false alarm but their sleep was ruined. Needless to say, Celia and Sarah turned straight over and went back to sleep. They have had more practice, what with being older.

By the time the two old codgers had surfaced, Dave and Daphne had been to two supermarkets and put the shopping away and Daphne was going out of the door on her way to her voluntary job.

Deciding I needed some fresh air, after lunch, I ventured out into the windswept garden… or what was left of it - the roses suffered badly, and Sarah was soon out there with her wretched camera. It's ok when she is taking photos of me, but who wants hundreds of pictures of a flower? Today was a videoing opportunity too.

What she is going to do with blurry videos of flowers in the wind I have no idea, but I will have to wait and see if she produces something worth looking at.

When I came in at teatime Daphne noticed that my right eye was looking a bit dodgy. It was half-closed and it looked as if I was winking, which I wasn't.

I kept out of the way as I didn't want anyone to pick me up and look any closer, but eventually it happened and I was swept off my feet without a word of warning and Celia bathed it with warm salty water.

I was then plonked down on the floor and left to do what I wanted to. Looking as if I was sleeping seemed a good idea, so I made my way into the lounge to recover my equilibrium.

Sarah decided to have another look at my eye, and tried to imagine how I had done something to it.

She reckons that while I was practising ballet in the garden, the wind had blown me over and that I hit my eye on something, falling in a very unladylike way, going from pirouette to resembling Pisa's leaning tower, then crashing down, which only shows what a fertile imagination she has. I am not going to reveal to anyone how it happened, it will just give them something to think about.

Having noticed the yellow rambling rose, which had such a profusion of flowers and buds when I was on a previous jaunt around the garden, I discovered that it had been torn down.

When Sarah came out later, she discovered the damage and decided to do something about it.

Armed with secateurs she cut off all the buds and blooms and filled a basket with them. She then thought it would be great to share them with the neighbours.

As Sarah is shielding and not supposed to go out, Celia, who was cooking their tea, agreed that if Sarah could run and put them on people's doorsteps and be back in time for tea in ten minutes that would be ok.

It was like playing knock down ginger, which they had played as children, where they had rung people's doorbells and then run away before the occupant could get to the door.

It was so enjoyable! Sarah hadn't had such fun for ages and got a great buzz from breaking the rules - she is so naughty!

After tea, Celia and Sarah disappeared into the lounge and I heard the whirring of the projector, so I knew what was coming: a film.

Oceans of sympathy swirled around and I was welcomed in to be with them and invited to sit on Celia's lap. Had I realised what the film was I would have had second thoughts.

As soon as it started, I knew I had made a *CATastrophic* choice, but I was feeling a bit poorly, at least I only had to watch it with one eye.

'The Sound of Mew-sick Live' was two and a half hours of awful singing. Not from the cast, but from my lovely companions who warbled, wobbled, and wrecked the evening. No wonder Dave and Daphne kept their distance.

I did like one song and felt it was rather apt for those of us who doss about: 'Idle Vice.'

Sympathy and concern meant I got into Sarah's bedroom where I hid under a chair until she had gone to sleep.

Then I took advantage of her comfy bed and while she deeply slept, I took my chance to have a quiet night at home to recover.

# 25TH MAY

Who said lockdown was boring?

I don't think I have ever seen anything as funny as Sarah trying to catch the mouse that I had brought into the house.

I'm sure I heard her say that visitors aren't allowed during lockdown, but it was only a very small mouse and I didn't think anyone would mind. They did!

Armed with a bucket and a dustpan, of course, she thought the mouse would be dead by the time she got to it, but it wasn't. It was quite a feisty mouse - she saw it in the garden, eyeing me up and defiantly trying to intimidate me.

The noise that came from her mouth was pretty spectacular too, a sort of strangled scream, which by rights should have terrified the mouse. She was grateful that only the mouse and I saw this extraordinary display, as everyone else was out.

When Celia returned, I heard Sarah shout 'Your cat has brought in a live mouse!' It's funny how I become someone else's cat when I have done something wrong.

Just like when Sarah had done something naughty and her mother would say to her father, 'YOUR daughter has just - - - -). Fill in with whatever action would be applicable e.g. drawn on the walls (she's always been creative,) fallen out of her dolls pram and broken her collar bone (she always was accident-prone) or refused to eat breakfast (she outgrew that).

I then found myself shut in the room they call the barn and I wasn't going to be let out until I had caught it.

Did I catch it? No of course not. Daphne and Sarah kept interrupting my snooze by tapping on the patio door and shouting 'Catch that mouse!'

Eventually, they gave in and let me out of the room.

In the absence of a humane mouse trap, Dave set a traditional one, shouting as he did it when it caught his fingers. The mouse was very canny and got the cheese off without disturbing the mechanism.

Up until that point it had been an idyllic sunny day.

It was a bank holiday and although he doesn't work in a bank, Dave was at home enjoying the opportunity to relax and spend some time with Daphne.

Sarah spent most of the day on her laptop or using her camera. Nothing changes there then.

Lunch was a help-yourself affair, obviously I wasn't included - I was expected to go out and catch my own treat if I wanted one. No muffins for me.

It should have been no muffins for Sarah too, but as it was a bank holiday, she had one for her lunch.

There are still eight left so we will have to see what excuse she can find today. I am sure she will think of something; as I've said before she's very creative.

Returning to the mouse, have you ever seen anyone dance the tarantella, it's a fast whirling dance? An old folk belief was that frenzied dancing was required after a tarantula spider bite.

It's actually a dance for two people, but Sarah certainly gave it all she had got and the rate that she spun and turned as she tried fruitlessly to catch the mouse was quite remarkable.

She certainly made up for the lack of a partner, I had never seen her with both of her feet off the ground at the same time.

She should go on Strictly Come Dancing. Another little surprise for you is Sarah's dancing skills, she can/could do ballroom and Latin American dancing.

One year on a cruise, a man said she danced like a bulldozer. Sadly, it was true, so her mother insisted that she had lessons, despite the cost.

She dragged along her best friend Linda and together they learnt to waltz, rumba and jive.

Well, they didn't dance with each other, there were a few men there to partner and as time went on, they progressed.

Despite her size Sarah is actually very light on her feet, when dancing, but not on the scales, please note she has lost a pound this week.

Her mother was a great dancer too, but she tended to try and dance the man's part, which caused ripples of mirth as her father asked if she had learnt to dance in a women's prison.

The next holiday came along and her mother thought her cajoling and scheming had paid off.

Sadly, once people found she could dance it seemed to have the effect of putting men off. All that money wasted and the hours of practice to no avail. Onboard ship you could have dancing lessons as every evening there was a dance in one of the ballrooms. Sarah went along just to keep in practice but caught the eye of the dancing instructor.

One evening when Sarah and her family were enjoying the music, they saw the dancing instructor go to the band and then held out his hand inviting Sarah to dance with him. The band broke out into a jive and he whisked her off her feet. As they started to dance, the floor emptied of the other dancers and like Danny and Betty Rizzo in the film Grease, they took the floor.

Her mother, who was also a Betty, said it was one of the proudest moments of her life. After tumultuous applause, Sarah returned to her seat and sheepishly grinned.

I have digressed.

Sarah spent most of the day on her laptop or using her camera. Nothing changes there then.

Everyone had their evening meal in the garden, someone mentioned Alf Fresco, but I didn't see anyone strange sitting with them, perhaps he's Sarah's imaginary friend Peter, who I mentioned on the ninth of May, but reinvented, into someone more in keeping with her age.

After telling you a highlight in Sarah's life, I have to tell you that once again she has no idea what she did last night after dinner.

Celia prompted her memory, Sarah rang her friends, Hilary, Julia, and Sam, and what a good time it was too.

What is she like.!

# 28TH MAY

The mouse is still at large, they even shut me in the room with it, but do you know what, I just couldn't be bothered to look for it.

Sarah suggested calling it Houdini, as it's a great escape artist. I personally think that's a stupid name for a mouse, especially as it's not a great escapologist, it's just that I can think of better things to do with my time.

Like what you ask? I could give you a list but that might be boring reading.

There's a box I have had my eye on for a few days, Sarah bought a food processor to replace their old one which had given up the ghost.

Daphne collected it from Sainsbury's, but when Sarah took it out of the box, she discovered it had a fault. They left it on the side in the kitchen, hoping it would mend itself I presume, but it hasn't. The box looks very comfortable and could become my next object to chew. There's nothing as satisfying as chewing lumps off boxes. Sarah said that's not true.

What does she know, I've never seen her try it! She might take it up as a new hobby, but she so rightly says she doesn't need a hobby and if she did, she has plenty of things to occupy her.

I did see some embroidery threads on her folding table and a box for them to go into. She says her table is actually called a butler table. She has just looked them up on the internet and hers is probably a 1920's one. A similar one had a chinoiserie design on it and was going for a lot of money. Hers has Fablon on it to make it easy to clean, so it's probably worth next to nothing.

She said it was at her dad's and when he died her sister offered it to her, so it's precious beyond words, as it reminds her of him, and happy times making things as they watched the TV together.

One memorable occasion was when Anna, his dog, a Weimaraner, came in rather bouncily and flicked her tail into Sarah's silk paint. This paint then went onto the Chinese wash carpet.

I wish I had been there to see her discreetly but manically removing it, it must have been quite a sight.

Celia said that Sarah is a dog lover really, but you could have fooled me.

I have just appeared beside her in the garden as I want to know what her response to this inflammatory statement is.

Rolling on my back I am waiting for her to stroke my tummy, I bet she couldn't do that and then say she likes dogs more than cats.

I thought so, she lasted about three seconds before she stroked me, actions speak louder than words.

That has knocked dogs off their pedestal.

She spent a long time yesterday weeding, whatever that is. She does it in the garden and pulls out plants and then wonders what to replace them with.

There are some small, mostly very small plants in the greenhouse. Still no sign of green, it's brown, perhaps she and Daphne are colour blind.

Anyway, a patch of garden by the pond is now empty and ready to be refilled.

Last night Celia shut me in the room with Houdini, but he evaded capture.

Since Lockdown started, Celia has been reading, books, not just cake recipes, which is good news and bad news. The bad news is she hasn't made any cakes, the good news is Sarah doesn't feel compelled to eat them. Well, it would be rude not too, but a present of muffins has filled the gap!

I think they are expecting me to take care of Houdini tonight.

Time will tell.

# 29th May

'Hurray, Hurrah and a budgerigar' is one of Sarah's little sayings along with, 'It's better than a slap in the belly with a wet fish' and 'You never get a second chance to make a first impression.'

This morning she is excited and I am the best thing since sliced bread, in some people's eyes.

I love getting lots of praise and treats. I am sure you have guessed: Houdini the mouse was found dead in the barn.

You may think, 'well you should expect rodents in a barn', which is true on a working farm, but our barn has been converted into a large sitting room with French windows and a bedroom and en suite.

It was designed as a granny flat, but Dave and Daphne don't want to be separated and she is the only granny here.

During the lockdown it has hardly been used but I think a change may be afoot.

I wonder why they say afoot? I would say *apaw.*

I have heard mutterings about bringing a table or two into the barn and abandoning the dining room.

Anyway, Houdini has gone to a resting place in the woods which added to the smiles on everyone's faces, except his.

Sarah wonders if losing a room will mean less to hoover. She has gone at it 'hammer and tongs' today but only did the downstairs rooms. She said the battery ran out on the hoover, a weak excuse if ever you heard one.

She seems full of idioms today which may need explaining to my overseas fans.

Back to 'Hammer and Tongs' I have seen no evidence of a blacksmith around here, hammering the metal that is held by his tongs. And certainly, no show of energetic activity unless Sarah trudging backwards and forwards to the kitchen making cups of tea counts.

In my opinion, it doesn't.

She says everyone needs to drink plenty in this hot weather, so I tried jumping to the top of the fountain, where a rude boy with no clothes on is hugging a fish. I nearly missed and Celia looked on and became very worried. If I hugged one of the fish I would be in great trouble, Sarah has just gone to check whether he has got any clothes on - the boy not the fish - in case her eyesight is failing.

He hasn't, and the fish spits water out into the pond. If I did that, I would be on a sticky wicket.

The day started with Sarah thinking I was asleep on her pillow. I wasn't. Her reversible brown and cream fleece had amazingly shaped itself into my profile, with a tail too. I wish I had been there to see her expression.

Not having a Ph.D. in origami made putting the faulty food processor back into its box a Herculean task, which after a lot of time, grunting, grumping and groaning, was thrust onto the Welsh dresser in a sorry state, as it seemed impossible to complete. A bit like a Rubik cube that she never finished either.

At eight o'clock some of the stalwart neighbours gathered in the street for the final NHS clap.

Sarah armed with her bugle gave it her best shot and made as much noise as she could.

A man on a bicycle rode through the throng trying not to look too embarrassed as saucepans and spoons, frying pans and cake tins were loudly thrashed.

After the clapping everyone returned to their homes and quietly got on with whatever they had been doing before their percussive outburst.

We will all miss our Thursday night contact, but when the lockdown is over, we will be able to say we took part in a piece of history in our own lifetimes.

Great-great-grandchildren will marvel at it, just like Sarah did when her great aunt Maud told her she had seen Queen Victoria's coffin paraded through the streets of London on its way to Windsor.

The evening was spent by Celia watching documentaries on her phone and Sarah looking at online art classes.

I wonder if she is planning to paint my '*Pawtrait*'?

# 30TH MAY

You know I said Sarah has had some imaginary friends in the past. Well, I have heard her talking to Victoria and Albert in her bedroom in the morning.

Not just one morning, but most mornings. I look around but there is no one there.

I do wonder if the lockdown has affected her, but sadly I think her royal friends were here before lockdown.

Fickle is a word I would use to describe my housemates. Yesterday, I couldn't put a paw wrong, today I am as popular as a fly in the ointment.

I lounged about trying to bask in yesterday's glory but memories are short.

It was another scorching hot day and Sarah continued her tapping away on her laptop, but eventually she felt she had done enough of that and went up to her bedroom to get her pencils and paper.

I was amazed that she actually came down with what she had gone up for. That is a rare occurrence - getting something from her bedroom involves getting distracted, popping into the bathroom, staring into space, not that there is much space in her room, opening drawers and cupboards. She then goes back downstairs and just as she gets back into the kitchen, she has a lightbulb moment and retraces her steps. If she is lucky, she will still remember what she was going for. If she doesn't, she will probably just go and do something else instead.

Out came her pencils and sketch pads. Making the first tentative steps is quite a challenge, deciding what size to do the drawing and which size sketchbook to use.

Decision made, well not exactly made, as she pulls out two sketchbooks and prevaricates between them, ultimately doing a sketch in each.

Yesterday she posted her A5 picture of me which I must admit gained a few likes. Today she says she is going to post her A4 sketch online.

She belongs to something called the Women's Institute which she really enjoys and is missing during the lockdown. She has made loads of friends there and goes to a couple of groups that are run by some of the members. She goes along with their walking group and they wander around local places and if they are lucky, finish near a café and then chat away and eat cakes. The calories burnt off by walking are far less than those consumed at the end, but she says it's all part of her effort to get healthy.

There's also an art group and Sarah loves going there and learning from Viv, who inspires and challenges them.

I have seen Viv in our house sometimes. she pops by for a chat.

Boy, do they chat!

I was very pleased with myself, as I managed to lose another collar. Sarah was disappointed because she had just drawn my picture including the detail on the collar, but she says not to worry as Celia has bought some more.

I hope you like the drawing I think it shows some of my regal bearing.

Oh yes, I forgot to tell you who Victoria and Albert are, you'll never guess!

Her hearing aids! Albert is the left one and Victoria is the right one. Once she went to the doctors, and her GP wanted to take her temperature with one of those digital thermometers.

'Hang on, I'll just take out Victoria.' Mystified, her doctor pulled the sort of face that is a combination of shock and incredulity.

# 31ST MAY

A case of mistaken identity.

Well would you know, my fame has spread far and wide.

Yesterday a post appeared on our neighbourhood page, from a lovely lady called Laura.

'I'm a new resident, I've noticed a black female cat with a white dot on her chest visiting me almost every day for over a week. She's very friendly. No collar. I was wondering if anyone has lost a cat matching this description?'

Amanda my friendly neighbourhood spy responded, 'Whereabouts on E Hunsbury do you live? It looks like Phoebe Furnackerpan.'

A photograph of my doppelganger then appeared. I must say what a beautiful cat. Shiny coat and a few white hairs on her chest just like me.

Sarah and Celia looked long and hard at the photo and they had to admit it did look just like me, they thought it even had a bit of a naughty look in its eye.

I looked at the photo later and couldn't believe that two such stunning cats could be alive on this planet at the same time and so close in proximity. Perhaps we are twins, I know nothing about my family or ancestors and Sarah said that census records only include people and not cats.

It turned out it wasn't me but a cat called Tokyo, perhaps we should become friends!

Next year I wondered if I could be included in the 2021 Census. Sarah found this entry in the 1911 one:

"The Rigby family of Upton Road, Birkenhead included their cat Tom in their census form.

'Tom Cat' was listed as being an 8-year old, married Mouse-Catcher, Soloist and Thief with 16 children. His birthplace was listed as Cheshire and he was described as being 'speechless'

in the infirmity section of the form.

The head of the household, William Rigby, obviously had a sense of humour as underneath he wrote, 'All the above mentioned have Breakfast, Dinner, Tea and Supper. Eat Standard bread Drink sterilised milk. Sleep with the windows open. Wash our Feet once a week etc.

God Save the King RSVP'. This, along, with Tom's details, was crossed out by an annoyed enumerator."

Of course, Sarah then got distracted and went onto a family history website to see if another Phoebe Furnackerpan existed, and to my delight it now proves that I am totally unique.

The nearest name was Phoebe Franklyn who lived in Boston America in 1646 with a very naughty husband. He exercised covetousness, pride and frowardness which is a word Sarah has never heard before. It basically means not easily controlled; stubbornly wilful, contrary.

Now who does that remind you of?

I have just jumped onto the table in the garden and peered around Sarah's laptop and then attempted to write my own definition of myself.

Kind, caring, compassionate, at least that sounds better than Mr Franklyn.

Sarah thought froward was more apt.

We will have words.

P.S. Many thanks to everyone on the neighbourhood page who care so much about cats.

# June 2020

I can see you.

# 1st June

As leisurely days go, this one was perfect and the sun shone incessantly. A gentle breeze wafted the warm air around the garden carrying the perfume of the roses and mice.

I think Sarah's sense of smell isn't as good as mine; she wasn't aware of the scent of the mice, which was a shame for her. I eventually pointed one out to her.

Dave was just coming out of the front door and unaware of me lying exactly where his foot needed to go. He stepped back with surprise and I grinned at him, but the smile wasn't returned as he struggled to retain his balance. He managed it and then stepped over me looking suspiciously at the drain pipe and the closeness of my nose to it.

Swiftly closing the door before him, memories of the previous mouse in the house loomed large and he didn't want a repeat performance.

Sarah watched from a distance, hiding behind her laptop. Celia opened the door. Sarah shouted at her to shut it quickly. Venturing out from behind her laptop Sarah armed herself with a broom, bravely knocked the drainpipe and a mouse ran up the wall.

I have heard of the expression climbing the walls, but that is usually connected to people.

Sarah moved amazingly quickly, back to the other side of the garden.

I took up my position on the doormat, alert and poised.

Celia was by this time on the wrong side of the door too, actually, I think being in the garden was the best side but she wanted to go back in.

Dave was in his bedroom and fortunately he heard Sarah call out and ask him to open another door so Celia could go back in.

Sarah took advantage of the opportunity and grabbed her camera.

Of course, once she had seen the mouse her fears were heightened and she looked decidedly jumpy. As she had got her camera out, I guessed she wanted to take some photos of me.

I rolled over on my back in my 'stroke me' pose, but she shouted at me, 'keep your eye on the mouse you vain creature!'

I complied and redoubled my search but suddenly the mouse made a break for freedom and Sarah zig-zagged across the cobbles.

I guided the mouse in her direction - I thought she would be pleased, people are so weird, will I ever understand them? Don't bother to answer that, we all know the answer.

The closer the mouse got the higher Sarah seemed to be off the ground, having stood on a concrete block. I was worried that she would leap onto the fountain edge and then fall in.

That would upset the fish, they don't like surprises.

Fortunately, she seemed aware of the possibility and put her feet resolutely back on firm ground.

What a palaver, she certainly got plenty of exercise. Thought I even detected a couple of rumba steps amongst her staccato moves.

Eventually I decided I had had enough of playing with Sarah and the mouse, and I wandered off.

Broom in hand Sarah tried to move the mouse which by now had died, but I wasn't very impressed so I ran back and took the mouse behind the hedge, eventually leaving it on the doormat where my game had begun.

Sarah returned to her writing and peace prevailed.

Everyone had watched Holy Trinity Brompton church in the morning so the day's usual pattern was different.

In the evening, Sarah could be heard by all and sundry, muttering - and I hate to tell you some of the mutters were a bit rude. I peeked over her shoulder as she sat tapping and grunting in the breakfast room. She was attempting to get all my posts into date order in a file on her laptop called 'Facebook Dates Phoebe,' having already abandoned the ones called 'The Daily Rant,' and 'Phoebe Book,' so with patience we will have to see whether she can manage it.

I won't hold my breath!

# 2ND JUNE

Wild would be an understatement, my behaviour didn't meet Celia's high expectations this morning.

A night out on the tiles meant that when I eventually came home, I was exceedingly skittish.

I must tell you that when Sarah is overtired, she gets very silly too. If she walks into a room clicking her fingers in time to a tune that only she can hear, beware, she is about to burst into awful jokes.

*Fur* example, what is the difference between a cat that got photocopied and a cat that follows you?

One is a cat copy, the other is a copycat.

Groan.

What do you call it when a cat wins first prize at a dog show?

A Cat-has-trophy!

Oh dear, I think Sarah may be a bit overtired too.

Still, she is sure that Trevor Saxby will share these with Clarence, but I suspect he has heard them before.

Enough frivolity, I must get on with my diary.

Exuberant describes well my behaviour this morning, I leapt from chair to table - got shooed off - chair to Welsh dresser - lifted off - from floor to the draining board– yanked off - from Celia's arms to front door – put down where Celia struggled to open it, then I made my escape back into the garden through the front door without using my cat flap. Objective achieved.

Who needs aerobics when I am around?

Today the shielding restrictions were relaxed, Sarah can now go out for a walk in the fresh air and meet a friend as long as they keep two metres apart.

She is allowed to do this once a day.

I would have thought she would be out dancing in the park or turning cartwheels.

I thought wrong, she seemed a bit overwhelmed by the idea, she says she's not alone, lots of people are feeling vulnerable about going outside and meeting friends.

No doubt she will overcome it soon, but she says she won't be doing cartwheels, as she has never been able to.

Plenty of time to learn, I would have thought, the lockdown isn't over. She says, 'you can't teach an old dog new tricks' but I don't really see what that has to do with my argument.

For starters, she is not a dog, she doesn't know any old tricks, unless you count touching her elbows behind her back. Her only qualification is being old.

It's a bit like Dave talking to his GP and asking, 'Will I be able to play the piano after the lockdown?'

The doctor shrugs his shoulders and says, 'Yes.'

'That's great,' replies Dave 'cos I couldn't play before!'

What was really stupid yesterday was that Sarah got up early to take part in a live online writing group. Then she forgot that was why she had got up earlier than usual.

She only remembered late in the afternoon.

Talking of the afternoon Celia got this idea that I should wear a harness. Can you imagine what that would do for my street cred? She had three main reasons, 1. I keep losing my collar 2. She thought I would like to coax Sarah to take a walk with a companion 3. She bought a harness cheaply a couple of weeks ago It's bright red too, it would have made a good video as I wriggled and writhed. They put it on upside down so that didn't help in the slightest.

I couldn't have walked anywhere with the lead between my back legs.

They got the message eventually and gave up.

I haven't heard Celia laugh so much for ages.

Mission accomplished, I slunk off for a sleep and spent the rest of the day dreaming of teaching the old codgers a few new tricks.

Finally, what do you call a cat that gets everything it wants?

*Purrsuasive!*

# 3RD JUNE

Naughty, me?

Never, don't you believe it, I stayed in last night, which means that I slept more, which means more energy to get rid of during the day.

Think giant parasol, breakfast in the garden, think sun glasses and hat.

Stunning weather, Sarah was out there and eating her breakfast before you could say muesli.

In fact, it was so hot she found it hard to concentrate on anything.

I was just the same, I moved around the garden, unable to settle.

Looking for places to lie in the garden is easy, they are plentiful.

In the summerhouse, underneath the apricot tree, behind the greenhouse, in the shade of a hedge… all seem tempting.

Sarah says I think I am the Marilyn Monroe of East Hunsbury, draping myself along the staircase or on Amanda's shed roof, or by the fountain.

When I want attention, which is often, I go into my Marilyn Monroe position, smile appealingly, with lips slightly apart and lay on my back awaiting to have my tummy stroked.

I don't think Marilyn would have wanted a tummy rub, but you never know what goes through people's minds.

I threw myself down in front of anyone who looked like they might pander to me.

Celia is an easy target, Sarah's not far behind, I'm not so sure about Dave and Daphne, but she did buy me some treats last week.

I was so desperate, at one stage in the afternoon I tried to drape myself almost under Celia's feet as she went down the steps into the kitchen but she didn't see me.

Sarah, who was watching as she peeled the vegetables, laughed out loud, (very rude!) as I entered the room head first with a startled look on my face.

Honestly some people have no manners.

I am afraid to tell you but as she is writing this, she keeps bursting into fits of laughter at the memory.

Very uncalled for.

It's her who always looks like something the cat dragged in. In fact, I think that's a bit unfair on cats.

You don't see her or Celia licking themselves all over to keep fresh.

Well, I haven't. I did lick Sarah's foot yesterday, it didn't taste too bad, but could have done with a bit more salt on it.

The idea that covering her foot in cat saliva doesn't appeal to her is strange. It's a sign of calm and bonding too.

Anyway, she needs a bit of grooming - take her fur for example, she has mountains of it on her head, in fact it goes halfway down her back, but doesn't grow on her back.

Thank goodness my fur isn't like that, if it was it would cost a lot to have it trimmed at the groomers, I don't think she's ever been to a groomer in her life.

Some pet groomers are offering to pick up people's pets during the lockdown. Perhaps they could take her away, as she has been in the house getting under my feet for weeks now.

I haven't tried licking Celia's feet, as I know she is a shy person and would probably get embarrassed.

I think I might try it, though perhaps it's something for me to do tomorrow and see how she reacts.

I was very spunky just before Sarah went to bed and chased up and down the back stairs trying to catch her hand as she put it through the bannisters.

I do hope I didn't over excite her as she will never sleep if she gets over excited.

I will see what she looks like in the morning.

# 4TH JUNE

Sarah says her brain is frozen, she really is a woosy.

She says who am I to talk, as I have dossed around all day, hogging the armchairs.

I don't like rain, horrible wet stuff, but Sarah says the garden needs it.

She didn't get out the garden hose either, one thing less to trip over.

Last time she went to put it away, she somehow got tangled in it.

When she first had her stroke, she got tangled in anything, especially getting dressed, and often tried to stuff both legs into one hole as she put on her trousers.

Don't mention fleeces, they were a nightmare, and even now she judges the day by how easily she can get dressed.

I am so grateful that I don't have to choose what to wear every day.

My only change of clothing is when I lose my collar and I have to wear a new one. Sarah thinks Celia should buy some shares in a cat collar company.

I don't really understand about the stroke, after all, I have a stroke every day - usually far more than one - and it hasn't made any change to my life.

Surely having a stroke is perfectly normal for a cat.

It reminded Sarah of when Tabby, their previous cat, was ill and Sarah went round to the neighbours and asked Andrew if he could lend them a cat basket to take her to the vets, as we thought she'd had a stroke. His answer was, 'Well our cat has a stroke every day,' which wasn't the expected reply.

He did find them a cat basket though.

Sarah has managed to shake off her writer's block during the lockdown and has finished writing her second book which will probably be called 'The Golden Seam – a Stroke of Genius.'

She says it's been writing my diary that has helped so much and the encouraging comments from people all around the world have given her more confidence.

One of the stories in the book is about when she had her stroke, how it felt, and its repercussions. She described her journey: 'Life breaks us, but if loving hands take us and we are prepared to let them mend us, out of our brokenness can come beauty. My life lay shattered, my sense of usefulness fragmented as if I had been a useful bowl which now was broken and lay scattered in shards on the floor.

Try as I might to get free, frustration had become my companion on this unasked-for voyage through troubled waters.

Kintsugi is the art of golden joinery in Japanese, and it refers to the process of fixing broken ceramics with gold. Chances are, a vessel fixed by kintsugi will look more gorgeous, and more precious, than before it was fractured.

Life breaks us in many painful ways. It's so easy to try and deny it, and disguise our cracks rather than let ourselves be seen as we are and then find the golden restoration that will make us more useful and valuable.'

She says she is about to start on what she hopes will be the final edit.

I can't remember if I have told you this before but she is very inspired by a saying. 'Don't curse the darkness – light a candle.'

I think she feels that she wants to spread light from her flickering candle to ignite hope in other people's lives.

Deep stuff tonight!

Wishing you sweet dreams.

Phoebe

# 6[TH] JUNE

Sarah had a headache so she has put yesterday's and today's entries together.

Everywhere I went for a sleep, the old codgers got in my way, and I moved around from chair to chair, as quick as a dog can lick a dish.

They were so annoying - they had got used to sitting in the garden for most of the day, and now they are under my feet all the time.

Sarah tried to cajole me to go out, she must have been joking, it was cold and damp.

It doesn't matter so much in the night, there's so much to occupy me, and I don't get disturbed.

Actually, I slept all day so, what with her headache and me dossing about there wasn't much to write.

I tell a lie, I have just remembered, while I snuggled down anywhere I could find, Sarah had a friend pop round.

I don't really understand why they sat outside, away from each other in the cold.

It didn't look that friendly, Sarah didn't give Penny a hug either, and when it started to rain, they sat in the summerhouse.

It's a beautiful place to snooze by the lawn, just a roof and poles with built-in benches and table.

They yawped on for ages, I watched from the warmth of the lounge, and they were still distant from each other.

Penny usually plays with me when she comes, but she never came into the house. That's never happened before.

After Penny left, Sarah was so cold that she had to go to bed and put on her electric fleece to thaw out.

Any old excuse eh!

She did get up for tea, hardly surprising really, and loafed about when she could have been taking dictation from me.

Yesterday was gloomy outside, but to cheer everyone up, I left them a gift at both doors.

At the backdoor a rather chewed mouse, well what remained of it. I thought I'd better leave them a bit and not be too greedy, and at the front door a shrew.

Sarah said it put her off her breakfast, but somehow, she managed to force down some yogurt and blueberries.

She then started doing her sums, I am sure I must have told you before that it's Sarah's least favourite form of torture, this activity is accompanied by copious amounts of tea.

Not to mention balls of paper flying across the room, hurled with oomph at the wastepaper basket, which she invariably misses.

Plus, lots of muttering, groaning and, far too often for my liking: rude words.

I do try to curl up into a tight ball if I am in the room so I am not polluted by her language and gesticulations.

I thought it was gloomy outside but it quickly became gloomy inside too.

One of the benefits of the lockdown is that she doesn't have to do her sums every week as they aren't spending as much money.

Sorting out the credit cards is the very worst job and Sarah got a gentle reminder from her lovely, patient friend Gail to prompt her to bring everything up to date.

Needless to say, she got stuck and gave up.

Then I managed to get some undisturbed sleep.

Despite a wind, the sun came out and cheered everyone up, especially Sarah who was able to escape into the garden.

She had plants to put in and was much less of a gloomy Eeyore and more like Tigger.

I heard tobacco plants being mentioned, which surprised me as I don't think of her as a smoker, and she is growing grass too on a bare patch of the lawn!

Weeding is still as mystifying as ever, pulling plants out and then putting new ones in, people are strange.

Talking of weed, she is laughing to herself as she remembered a nice girl who came to stay.

The girl asked what was for lunch and Sarah replied: 'Roast potatoes, vegetables, and a joint.' You should have seen the look on the girl's face!

Daphne suggested watching a film last night. They took ages to choose one and of course, they opted for the one that was first mentioned.

I sat on Celia's lap for a bit, but Sarah was sorting out her embroidery silks in the dark! Winding them onto small cards and popping them into a box.

This unheard-of act of organisation on her part became a game I thought would be fun to join in, sadly I wasn't welcome, so to show my disgust I draped myself over a box of Maltesers that was on the coffee table. They were rudely snatched away, so I gave up and bedded down in a bean bag for the rest of the film.

I haven't heard Celia laugh so much for ages, I had no idea she could laugh so loudly and for such an extended time. I wish we had got one of those machines that measure decibels, but she would have probably broken it.

Sarah nearly took her hearing aids out, but as there were no subtitles, she decided against it.

They went off to bed in a jolly mood and I sneaked out for another night on the tiles.

# 7th June

Sarah seems to spend ages washing her hands over and over again, and when she is doing her twenty second hand washing, she sings the Owl and the Pussy Cat.

I thought you ought to know.

That wasn't all Sarah did yesterday, I think she may be a bit under the weather, and by that, I mean rain and fog, not sun and blue skies.

She has been watching 'The Hotel Inspector' with Alex Polizzi, well, not watching it with Alex in her bedroom, watching her in it, but this has had a good effect on Sarah.

Tidying her bedroom usually indicates depression, a high temperature, or a bout of delirium.

Anyway, Alex has inspired Sarah to get a grip after watching her programme.

Not that we live in a hotel - my friends are never given a warm welcome when they come Into the house. I think Alex would tell Sarah to smarten up, be a bit more professional, and greet them politely. 'Hello Chubby Checker, how lovely to welcome you to our house today.

Would you like me to show you your room?'

This is instead of the wild banshee shouts of 'Chubby Checker, what are you doing in the kitchen? Get out at once.'

I feel quite hurt sometimes. I know they aren't welcoming anyone into our home at the moment, but it hasn't always been like it is now.

Normally, everyone would be welcomed with open arms, teas and coffees poured, meals prepared, the more the merrier.

Tuesday evenings there used to be ten at least for the evening meal, often even more on a Thursday evening, a few people for tea on Saturday and a crowd of people for Sunday lunch. Lockdown has stopped all that. Now there's just the five of us to feed, and I have special food because I am special.

Celia diligently feeds me four times a day: 'little and often' said the vet. I wouldn't want to have to rely on Sarah with her memory loss to guarantee regular meals, Dave and Daphne would be a safer option.

A few people have talked in the garden, standing at least six feet apart, but now the weather is colder it's not as appealing.

Cornettos and individually wrapped ice-creams are offered instead of a hot drink, but not many people want to stand in the cold with an ice cream. Celia and Sarah would - nothing puts them off. Sarah has been known in the depth of winter, on a trip to her home town, to eat a tub of Rossi's ice cream inside a parked car watching the waves break on the shore. Even her friend's dog, Bertie Thomas, had his own ice cream that day.

Sarah noticed, when she was away in Wales, that shops now sell ice cream for dogs. Old sock flavour would be a favourite I should imagine.

Maple bacon is on offer, and *pawsecco* freeze pops can be enjoyed by cats and dogs, lickers, and chewers.

I would like shrew and mouse flavours, sprinkled with duck treats and salmon sauce.

Cats don't have sweet taste receptors, so I wouldn't appreciate salted caramel and toffee and I'm lactose intolerant so it needs to be made using goat's milk or kitten milk.

I bet you didn't know you that you can get kitten milk! Cow's milk comes from cows, but kitten milk doesn't come from kittens, it's specially manufactured to be the same as a mother cat's milk which is obviously the best thing for us.

I doubt that Celia will buy me any, but she is much more generous than Sarah, so if I need to appeal to anyone it will be her.

I do hope friends will be able to come around soon, that would cheer everyone up.

Another interesting fact I came across is that pet shops sell far more cat collars than toys.

Which brings me neatly onto the fact that I have lost another one!

Eventually, someone may pick up the hint that I don't like wearing them, but Celia says for the sake of the birds I need to have a bell attached to me somewhere.

Honestly, it makes me feel more like a leper than a 'daring do' leopard who is a distant cousin of mine.

Last night everyone ate in the dining room and had a Chinese meal, everyone except me, of course.

Although I did have duck, but not rolled in pancakes with jam stuff in it.

Still, I can't complain, I am loved, and that's the most important thing in life.

P.S. Sarah's room looks a bit better.

# 8th June

Sarah has absolutely no idea what day it is and is resorting to asking Alexa in the morning, but the chances are that by the time she has got downstairs she has already forgotten.

Sarah that is, not Alexa, who is a bit of a know all.

I find her a bit infuriating if I am totally honest, you only have to say her name and she's there ready to give you the right answer.

She should take lessons from me, I pretend I am deaf or asleep, but really, I don't want to be bothered.

It's very annoying when I get prodded, and Sarah thinks I should be doing something that would wear me out in the daytime.

Last night I hid at bedtime, actually, I was very cross, because Celia had tried to block the cat flap again, so I thought I'd leave her to worry. Sarah had spotted me in the spare room, sulking, I faced the wall and wouldn't even acknowledge her presence.

I got Celia up at four-fifteen! I wanted to go out. Wouldn't have stood a chance with Sarah, by the time she's taken her glasses off she can't even read the time on her alarm clock radio.

Hearing aids out too, and you might as well throw in the towel, poor old dear, The day had started well, Celia got up again and gave me my breakfast and went back to bed Being Sunday I knew the routine that everyone would have, and sure as eggs are eggs, everyone bundled into the lounge at eleven and Sarah hitched up the laptop to the projector.

This can sometimes have the same effect as doing sums, but today she succeeded fairly quickly with no rude words.

I am fairly discerning about what I watch with them, but I must admit I do enjoy Holy Trinity Brompton Church @home.

I stayed in all the way through sitting politely on Celia's lap.

After lunch Celia made oodles of phone calls, yapping away to all and sundry, I have no idea what she finds to talk about for so long, I guess it must be about me.

She made a new discovery today: I like the taste of soap. I try to pick it up with my paws and then lick it off. Sarah has no idea why, but her stomach churns at the very thought of it.

It reminded her of when a friend's daughters gave a joke sweet that tasted of soap to a friend of ours. He just ate it and the girls thought that it was a waste of their pocket money.

Some years later he recalled the experience and said it had tasted odd, like soap, but he ate it anyway.

Sarah is practically frothing at the mouth just thinking about it.

She has said she is going to be doing sums tomorrow, which is always a strain for us all. I think I will go to bed and keep out of her way.

She did watch a bit more of 'The Hotel Inspector' tonight, but whether it has the desired effect upon her, is anybody's guess.

Watch this space!

# 9TH JUNE

The sun is shining today so Sarah can sit and write in the garden, that gives me the whole house to find a comfy spot in.

Well not the whole house, but most of it.

In ancient Rome a cat was a symbol of liberty, I am always taking liberties so I am a purrfect example of a cat.

I was in a restless mood yesterday, makes a change from saying naughty, but it amounts to the same thing!

After a long night out I returned home exhausted, which means I could be in either of two moods: belligerent and grumpy, or fulfilled and happy.

When I am fulfilled it may have something to do with being filled full of mice and shrews.

Sarah can't believe how many I leave as gift offerings, but I do eat more than they know about.

A bit like Celia and Sarah and ice cream. Their latest excuse is, if someone comes round (as they can't invite them in because of lockdown, or offer them a hot drink), ice lollies come individually wrapped so are hygienic to share.

They have got some ice lolly moulds too from the nice man at Amazon, and are going to make some elderflower cordial lollies and fat free yoghurt ones.

I wonder if they will make me some tuna flavoured ones, or even ice cubes, some cats appreciate something nice to help them cool down?

I hope they realise you have to use tuna packed in water not oil, if you pop in a few cat treats they are like chocolate chips in the old codgers' ice cream.

Sarah says you must wash out the ice tray very thoroughly afterwards as she doesn't like the taste of fish.

I suggested asking the man from Amazon to get me a special cube tray. You can get them made of silicone in different shapes, I wonder if they make mouse shaped ones?

Sarah has just got distracted and started looking at cat ice trays. For £3.50 you can get one with cat shapes.

She has now discovered a silicone mice mould, which doubles up for ice or jelly or sweets.

Now that really sounds fun.

Nice, iced, mice, *purrfect.*

They are on offer, buy one get one half price, they could keep one for me and one for them to fill with chocolate.

I don't know what gin is but it seems to go with ice, well it does in the adverts.

Celia has just announced that she has been eating up all the salt and vinegar crisps, as Dave and Sarah don't like them. That's what I admire in Celia - she is a very sacrificial person.

Now Sarah has googled 'top tips for keeping your cat cool in summer.' It says cats can feel hot and bothered and can suffer heatstroke. Making them ice lollies with tuna in brine or low-salt chicken stock for an icy snack will help keep them entertained and cool.

Playing with ice cubes is fun too, and helps cool down their paws if you put them on a hard floor.

You can get cooling mats but a freezer block wrapped in a small wet towel can work wonders.

Celia must keep my water bowl filled up at all times, and people must be careful not to shut us into sheds or greenhouses.

If I did get shut in a shed, it said on the internet that I might get lethargic and confused – a bit like the old codgers then.

I must make sure Sarah doesn't spend too long in the greenhouse as she is confused enough as it is.

Grooming ourselves helps keep us cool too, our saliva evaporates off our fur and helps cool us down, so do remember that next time you stroke a cat!

I am off to find somewhere comfy to have a nap.

Adios amigos.

# 10th June

I felt very lethargic today after another busy night.

Sarah and I have been gardening and I so enjoyed her help.

She wasn't as keen as I was and she really got under my feet, not to mention planting flowers in the very bit of garden which I had decided would make a wonderful outdoor litter tray.

I have said this before, on more than one occasion, that I get muddled about weeing and weeding.

She had turned over all the soil in a bed near the fountain. I still believe beds are for sleeping in, but Sarah says 'woe betide me' if I sleep on her new plants.

That's a rather old-fashioned expression, she could just have said 'Beware bad things may happen to you if you sleep/sit/walk/gambol on my new plants.'

She can be a bit old fashioned at times, but on the whole, she is fairly up to date with things people say, well she likes to think she is!

I had great fun being with her, but she went off into the house for something and I took this as my opportunity to establish myself as the head gardener. She had been listening to Radio 4

playing on her phone and left it on the stones by the bed.

This was my chance to have a close up look at it and a listen in. It was fascinating, how do all those people get into such a small box?

So many of them too and they were telling us all the day's news, as it was six o'clock.

When she came back out to carry on with the planting, she went to kneel on her kneeling stool, but I got there first, after all, it was the only comfy cushion in the garden. I refused to get off. I gave her my imperious look, trying not to look arrogant and domineering; just regally entitled to be there.

It didn't work and she shoved me off.

Sitting on the earth isn't always very nice.

Anyway, I had the last laugh when I pooped just where she was planning to dig!

# 11th June

What a grey day. Sarah seemed very subdued, perhaps she had been up all night like me.

Eeyore comes to mind, I don't think she means to be like him, but there are similarities.

I danced about the room between naps, like a red balloon, trying to cheer her up; it was hard work being a balloon.

I don't think it worked either, which was a shame, as I put a lot of effort into it.

She didn't get up until it was almost my lunchtime, I don't know what a headache is but I hope it's not catching.

She can't write much about the morning due to not being awake, although I did hear her say she had a dream where her friend Penelope Ashby was a spy.

Trying to disguise herself, Penny popped a couple of olives under her eyelids. It was scary to see her with green pimento stuffed olives where her eyeballs should have been. Sarah freaked out and said she looked frightening.

Penny then decided to try something different and went for black olives the next time, saying 'Perhaps they will think I am blind.'

I don't know what Sarah's response was or who they were spying on, but it sounded as if some colourful encounters might be in store.

Just before she woke up, she and Penny were doing something with a very long zip and telling someone how to survive and get air if they were hiding under a lawnmower.

It was in glorious technicolour.

I wasn't in the dream so it can't have any significant or deep meaning.

Sarah did disappear back to bed for a bit in the afternoon, I wasn't invited, so I sulked on the armchair and then she reappeared to cook everyone's tea.

I don't know what curry is but it smelt quite different to what she normally cooks.

Living with short term memory loss, she finds cooking a challenge, but the curry was a success - she did wander off and forget it was on, but it didn't taste too burnt!

It's the executive functioning part of her brain that is damaged, so following instructions or reading a book are difficult to do.

Modern technology is so helpful. If she forgets where she is, or how to get home, she's a dab hand with her phone and Google maps.

Of course, she has now gone off to find out what a 'dab hand' is. It probably comes from 'dab' in the sense of 'touch lightly'.

As well as Google she has got Brewers Dictionary of Phrase and Fable, which her creative writing instructor said was a good source of enticing nuggets and information.

She misses him a lot. He died last year of oesophageal cancer and she spoke at his funeral. She felt it was such an honour to be asked, and is sure that he would enjoy reading my diary.

There are lots of little things that remind her of him as she writes. What a legacy he has left behind: writers who are doing the business, and walking the walk.

Although their friendship was brief, it was precious. He had started mentoring her, with the aim of her teaching creative writing and to use it, particularly to help those living with memory loss, dementia or stroke-related issues.

She went to bed much earlier than usual and watched 'The Hotel Inspector', at which point I went out to explore in the dark and rustle up a snack or two.

# 12th June

Sarah is always waffling on about how amazing technology is.

Today I had a chance to experience it for myself!

I just can't imagine how Sarah can talk to a group of people, all at the same time, in different places all over the world, but she can.

She was still a bit subdued, but after breakfast, she settled at the table, with one eye on the weather and one eye on me.

Wasn't she clever to be so good at multi-tasking, has she got three eyes? Actually, I think she might have eyes in the back of her head. If I am doing something that she thinks I shouldn't do, she always catches me. Sarah's mother had eyes in the back of her head too, so it must be a genetic gift. Sarah used to throw all the books that were in the bookshelves in the lounge over her shoulder when she was a toddler. Her mother always caught her doing it. I can assure you that she now has a healthy respect for books, lots of them.

These days her mother could have a video baby alarm or an indoor security camera and keep her eyes on Sarah, her sister and the dog without ever leaving the kitchen.

Sarah thinks it would have been ghastly, and so do I.

After reviving herself with a mug of tea, there was a strange noise coming from her portal. It's a screen where people can talk to Sarah, or Celia, or anyone who happens to be in the room. Grabbing a chair and yelling for Celia, she hit the magic button, and her friend Mark appeared.

Goodness me did they chat, I ear holed the conversation, and some of it was about me! Mark is a journalist and Sarah was asking him for advice on whether to publish my diary.

They certainly covered a wide range of subjects from house prices, what the result of the lockdown will be, next up was dementia, and Sarah hopes that the ideas she suggested will be useful. She said that some museums do special tours and many cinemas throughout the country now offer dedicated dementia-friendly showings.

Sounds a bit like our lounge, there is a big screen and a projector, and you can come and go as you like.

I do that anyway, especially if I think the film is boring and not my cup of tea.

Next up was a call from some of her college friends, I was going to say 'old friends' but I thought they might be a bit touchy. Their conversations were quite frivolous to begin with, as they talked about there being no public toilets open during the lockdown. I couldn't see what the fuss was all about, I go whenever and wherever I want to, including as mentioned yesterday, in the flower beds where Sarah is gardening.

Have you ever thought why gardening is called gardening, but you don't say you are housing when working inside? Not everyone lives in houses, so you might be bungalowing, or flating or maisonetting.

Anyway, back to the subject, there were hoots of laughter as they discussed their different dilemmas: some of them weren't very observant when it came to crouching behind a bush - stinging nettles were mentioned - they should be like me and take note of their surroundings carefully. Sarah said she has written a short story about incontinence, which she feels is an unmentionable subject, but when it is talked about, everyone realises they're not alone. When she read it at a Women's Institute, many said if they weren't incontinent when they came, they were by the time the story was finished!

How amazing to know that people could see me on the other side of the world. Yolanda was in Barbados. Pat was in America, and Sonya in Brussels, not to mention the rest of them in the UK.

Sarah picked me up and let me wave to everybody, and I was unusually still as I sat on her lap.

Don't worry I will make up for lost time!

Fancy someone in America seeing me! They are very lucky. Sarah's white hair was commented on and the fact that they nearly all wore glasses. Good job too, it would be a shame if I was on their screen and they couldn't see me clearly. Sarah is as blind as a bat without her glasses.

Everyone talked about lockdown and what they have been doing during it.

In a typically British way, they talked about the weather, one hundred and thirty degrees in America, but they do have air-conditioning and that's in Fahrenheit, thirty degrees that's eighty-six in old money in Barbados, but the hurricane season is just about to begin, so perhaps I should be grateful.

Talking to people she hadn't seen for forty-five years although strange, was fun, and she cheered up a bit, and then went and potted up some geraniums to go in the urns by the front door.

The evening passed pleasantly, Sarah was drawing a portrait of me, it is still a work in progress, just like me.

# 13th June

I started the day in the manner I meant to carry on in. Naughty!

First thing, when Celia and Sarah eventually appeared. they looked a bit dishevelled - well Sarah usually does - I pranced around the breakfast room.

As soon as Celia had opened the cupboard where the glasses and pudding bowls live, I eyed it up.

'Mmm,' I thought, 'Haven't been in there before,' and a very wicked idea entered my head, well not exactly wicked, more mischievous with a hint of bravado slipped in. A bit like Eric Morecambe when he was about to play a trick on Ernie Wise. If I wore glasses, I would have lifted them up as I made my exit behind the curtain.

Nothing wrong with my eyesight, just to assure you I can spot a shrew a mile off.

Returning to the cupboard, just as Celia turned her back, I sprang into action and leapt up into it, despite there not being much space to put a paw down. Let alone four.

Sarah became a bit, well, what shall I say, screechy: 'Get down you rapscallion feline!' Blimey, she must have swallowed the dictionary for breakfast, and then I realised she hadn't had her yogurt and fruit yet. 'Get down' doesn't appear in my dictionary so I looked at her blankly. It was a tight squeeze perching myself precariously amongst the dishes. I had to curl my tail over to fit in, but I managed, pulling a belligerent face as I did so.

Eventually Sarah's strong hands grabbed me. Kicking and wriggling I was removed from the cupboard with a ferocity I hadn't expected.

And that was just the start of the day!

Celia went out to meet a friend for a social distancing walk and then made a long overdue visit to the bank.

Sarah faffed about writing and googling, and then when the sun came out, she went into the garden and put some more plants in.

She loves planting things and nurturing them. She is deadly with indoor plants - they take one look at her and lose the will to live.

She has lovingly grown zinnias, cosmos, and snapdragons from seed, along with dwarf rudbeckia, cleome, and runner beans.

I had better not sit on any of them or my name will be mud.

Our lovely friend Sonya turned up in the garden later and there at the table by the pond they all sat and chatted. I knew it wouldn't be long before ice cream would be mentioned and almost on cue, Celia offered to make the sacrificial journey to the freezer.

I don't get it this obsession with it, perhaps if they gave me some I would understand. I must do my Marilyn Monroe impression and see if they succumb to my charms.

Whatever ice cream is, they seem very possessive about it, and despite me throwing myself down in front of them, they didn't share a single crumb.

Sarah has since pointed out that you don't get crumbs of ice cream, bits that fall off are blobs. I think she would have licked her arms if any blobs got on them.

Talking of blobs, she is chuckling away remembering when she and her dad and Lucy went for an ice cream cornet at Southwold beach.

He kindly treated everyone, and Lucy and Sarah started licking theirs but his immediately melted and ran down his arms.

Sarah was beside herself with laughter, she can be very cruel when it comes to other people's misfortunes. I am sure if it had been her cornet, she wouldn't have seen the funny side of it!

I will be very attentive next time they have ice cream.

# 14th June

Well I had the house to myself this afternoon.

Sarah hasn't really been out since the start of lockdown, as she is shielding, so a trip to the Harrold Odell Country Park was a welcome outing.

That of course was the equivalent of when the cats away the mice will play!

They will never know what I got up to, but they have vivid imaginations.

I couldn't get into Dave and Daphne's rooms, but if any doors had been left ajar, I took advantage of the situation.

Sarah has got a lovely duvet in a cover and after I've pummelled it a bit and got it into a nest shape, it's luscious and perfect for a peaceful nap.

She doesn't usually leave her bedroom door open, so when the opportunity pops up, I grab it with both paws.

She took loads of photos while she was out. It made a change for her to photograph something other than me.

A swan opened its wings and she said it felt as though creation was welcoming her back.

Can't say I felt as enthusiastic as that when she returned and I got turfed off the bed.

I went off in high dudgeon and stayed out until it was my tea time.

When it was their tea time I presented them with a live mouse, I thought it might supplement their meagre diet.

What a hoo-ha ensued. Sarah managed not to jump on the table, Celia sat put, and said, 'Sarah shut that door,' and gallant Dave picked up the backdoor mat with the mouse in it and plonked it outside. I felt very affronted, I thought it would go with sausages but sometimes my kindness is just not appreciated.

Sarah seems a bit obsessed with digging holes and putting in plants, but she was tempted away from her task by a piece of carrot cake. It doesn't take much at all to divert her.

Side-tracked completely, she then started loading her new photos onto her laptop.

She ignored me after that. So, I went back into the garden with my tail raised high and my nose in the air.

I didn't even come and join them when they settled down to watch a film together. I heard Celia laughing and laughing and laughing.

It must have been a good film, turned out it was called 'We're Not Angels', more than appropriate in my humble opinion.

I stayed out all night, that'll show them.

# 16TH JUNE

Another glorious day, Sarah spent most of it in the garden. She was going to do some gardening but her mouth got in the way.

What I am trying to say is that she talked most of the day. She and Celia spent the afternoon with their friend Janice.

Of course, this progressed into an opportunity for ice cream!

I was right too about Sarah, but then I usually am - she did get a blob of ice cream on her arm and she did lick it off.

She is a slow learner, but I am glad she has paid attention to my habits, and is slowly learning and practising them.

Planting was neglected again, honestly when will she get it all together, but it did mean that her bed was free and I made good use of it.

You would have thought by now that she would remember to close her bedroom door.

Early on in the day she seemed a bit depressed, that black dog was on the prowl, but she said talking helped, that and the sunshine. Not only did she talk a lot to Janice, she also spoke to people on the phone too.

She chuntered on about my diary and I heard her talk about possibly getting it published, so the evening was spent researching various options.

If she gets an agent and publisher it could take months if not years by which time hopefully lockdown will be a distant memory.

Faster possibilities include self-publishing with Amazon but she will need help, or using a small publishing company who can get it up and running quickly but that costs a fair amount of money. Or using a crowd funding site for authors.

Decisions, decisions.

It kept her so occupied she didn't know I had bedded down for a snooze on her bed.

Celia went shopping in the morning and in the afternoon went to exchange the car, changing over to an automatic. Gone is the shiny red one and the new car is smaller, more economical and will be a great help, as Celia has Arthur Ritus in her hands.

Arthur has appeared in my diary before. I have never seen him but Celia says he is always there. Sarah knows him too.

The old codgers had a pleasant and quiet evening, I tried not to disturb them.

Finally, I must tell you about my experience in Sarah's bedroom.

I tried getting into Sarah's wardrobe and she asked, 'What are you doing?' I replied 'It's "Narnia Business".'

Think Sarah is probably overtired, so I will sign off now, before she gets too silly.

# 17th June

I tried being extra well behaved and helpful today.

Sarah had great plans for today, and as Robbie Burns said 'the best laid plans of mice and men often go awry.'

I must admit I have scuppered the plans of quite a few mice since I took up residence here.

I put 'took up residence' as it sounds a bit posher than being brought here in a cat box with no idea where I might end up.

Fortunately, I chose well when the old codgers came to present themselves for consideration at the RSPCA open evening.

Sarah said it reminded her of Harrod's sale: lots of people all trying to get the same thing. But what it really meant was lots of cats all trying to choose their new owners at once.

Needless to say, Sarah and Celia thought they were choosing their cat, and two others they looked at were snapped up before they had a chance to say which one they wanted.

Can you imagine them having a calico cat who Sarah had already chosen a name for, 'Tinkerbell,' or a ginger cat called 'Montmorency, Edward Sheeran.'

They both were quick movers and avoided getting embarrassing names by choosing their owners straight away when they saw the old codgers in the queue to view.

Sarah had certain things she had in mind for a perfect cat:

1. It shouldn't have been a stray as it might have picked up bad habits. Getting on the kitchen work surfaces to scavenge food, sprung to mind.
2. She really wanted a tiny kitten so she could train it.
3. She has a partiality to ginger cats.

I really fitted the bill *purrfectly*.

1. I was a stray, who was street wise.
2. I had already had kittens of my own.
3. She had never entertained the thought of having a black cat.

I picked them because Sarah had a kind face, her dad always said her face was enough to make a cat laugh, and it did!

She appealed to my sense of humour, amusing but never catty.

Celia, well she was a pushover, and I thought I could wrap her around my little finger.

You never get a second chance to make a first impression!

Celia immediately said yes, she would be happy to be chosen by me and signed some papers.

Sarah initially looked a little disappointed, but I have exceeded her expectations, in more ways than one.

I knew what I was getting, just didn't know where I would end up living.

I must say this is a first-class establishment. Sarah has been watching 'The Hotel Inspector' and she thinks Alex Polizzi would approve, but would make a few recommendations to improve my rooms.

Starting with my bedroom, she would suggest taking out the washing machine and tumble drier and replacing them with a water fountain and with soundproofing.

Sarah's singing is in a word, ghastly, and Celia sings along to the radio, so that's not too restful.

Also get rid of the bin that Celia sometimes puts in front of my cat flap, when she is trying to make me stay in. Alex would suggest some really super comfortable armchairs, to replace my barely comfortable ones. and put one in each room so I never had to slum it.

These would be for my exclusive use, like the one in the breakfast room.

Sarah went out into the garden this afternoon and I thought I would help her.

I am not too sure how she felt about that.

She was digging plants out of the garden and putting new ones in, I just don't get it.

Why would you do that? I heard her say 'a rose in a cabbage patch is a weed,' if you don't want it there.

Whichever patch of the garden I was trying to be helpful with, she seemed to be in my way, but she intimated it was me that was in her way.

How's that for gratitude. In the end I decided to have a nap under a large leaf, yes it was pretty huge compared to most other leaves I have seen.

Not as big as the Acanthus which has developed mould, or the Artichoke which is massive. Sarah says she wonders whether it is a true artichoke or a silly bum thistle.

She can be very rude.

As a rule, she is usually self-controlled, although she has got a bit of a reputation otherwise, but I'd better not dwell on that.

As I was trying to relax and have a nap, she kept saying things like 'Don't you dare knock over my cosmos!' (Whatever a cosmos is I'm not too sure).

Then to make matters worse she got out her wretched camera and tried taking photos of me at lots of different angles, not just one or two but loads.

She knelt down, crouched down, hovered over me, got in close, stood away and zoomed in. Really, she is taking liberties, as well as photos!

I think the only thing she didn't do, but is famous for, is laying down to take a picture.

She does that sort of thing in cathedrals, and at National Trust gardens, anywhere she can embarrass her friends.

I think having listened to her groaning as she gets up, that perhaps she wasn't up to it, or should I say down to it!

Eventually there was a massive downpour which started just after she had gone in to cook the tea.

She spent the evening looking at which publishers had already brought out books written from an animal's point of view.

And rounded off the evening with a cheery dose of 'The Hotel Inspector.'

# 18TH JUNE

Social dis-dancing. The very name makes me nervous.

Dancing is a dangerous sport, especially for cats.

Sarah used to go disco dancing in her dim and distant past, but she never really enjoyed it.

I do think it sounds like some kind of dance. The sort you might do at a barn dance perhaps.

A social dis-dance, I guess. Can't imagine Sarah and Lesley bopping away, but I do happen to know they went to a David Bowie Tribute act just before the lockdown.

I'm sure they shimmied a bit, I also know they made the mistake of standing near the Gents, which was a bit inconvenient, convenient for the men but not for our dynamic duo.

There are sadly no photos to show you of her in her heady student days, I guess if mobile phones had been available, there would have been lots of shots of her jiving, twisting and contorting her body.

Nowadays, just putting on a fleece top can be a triumph: same movements, older body.

Back to the topic in hand. Lesley, Sarah's friend who is very clever at making things, came for a social distancing chat in the garden.

Fortunately, the drizzle had stopped by the time she arrived and they were able to have a chat in the fresh air.

It had been so long since they had seen each other. Normally they meet up every week, but this was their first time since lockdown.

Lesley's hair had changed colour twice, and Celia soon arrived on the scene and asked if anyone would like some ice cream.

I bet you can guess the answer!

Anyway, Sarah says ice cream is bad for cats, but I think it's just so there is more for her.

She googled it, so it must be true.

She gets very easily distracted on Google and scarily she also found videos about training cats, I do hope her memory will fail her and that I don't have to suffer her throwing balls at me or getting me to dance on my hind legs. Very undignified in my opinion and the clothes they had to wear! All ribbons and bows and teeny jumpers, not my style, on any day of the week.

Back to Lesley, she didn't stay long, none of Sarah's friends do these days. I think it must be something to do with the lockdown.

Although she has used a different deodorant, but it's not that.

Normally Lesley would stay for at least six coffees and lunch, but an ice cream was on the menu and that was all.

I do hope she made it home ok, I hate to think of her starving on the return journey.

# 19th June

Sarah has been zooming around today.

She's usually quite slow, so I was a bit surprised, but amazingly she never left the table.

Talk, talk, talk, never stopped, hardly drew breath, well I exaggerate, she did stop to make cups of tea and eat.

The East Hunsbury WI were having a trial run at having a zoom meeting online, and Sarah was the guest speaker.

She does write about a lot of topics, even I thought the story she read was very funny. It was about incontinence, which is no laughing matter. It's one of those things people struggle with, and never mention.

Then if someone owns up to suffering with it, you find you're not alone, in fact you are part of a club, which you would rather not belong to.

It's the same when you lose your parents, you join a club of orphans, but rarely acknowledge it.

What nobody knew was I was hiding under the cushions in the lounge, out of sight with my ears pricked up.

It took a while to get everyone online and active, but Sarah said it was worth the effort.

How great to see those smiling faces again! The one thing they all talked about was being in the queue for the hairdresser.

They didn't look too bad, but imagine being number three hundred on the list, or did I hear seven hundred and six.

Fortunately for me, I don't need to go anywhere to get a fur cut, I just lick mine into shape.

I wouldn't want to attempt to lick Sarah into shape, she has so much hair I could get lost in it.

Rumour has it, that on one visit to the hairdressers, he found her school beret buried deep inside!

She hasn't always had long hair. As a child, her mother made her have it cut like Julie Andrews in the 'Sound of Mewsick' and she used to sellotape Sarah's fringe to her forehead, in an effort to control it after she washed it. You should have heard her scream when the Sellotape was pulled off.

When she was old enough to go to the hairdressers on her own, she had it cut very fashionably – crew cut with a spot of elf, think Mia Farrow when she cut off all her hair to annoy Frank Sinatra.

Sarah loved it but her mother cried for days. Her father said 'if you ever do that again, don't darken my door.'

A rare moment of teenage rebellion rose up and of course, she did it again.

Not long after leaving the WI zoom group, she got a video call from a 'girl' she had been at college with and they had a great chin wag.

She did get some lunch and then at three she zoomed again with her classmates from college.

From the far corners of the globe, they chatted. Reminiscing about pubs, and counting up their grandchildren. And all agreeing that they were the same people inside as they were at nineteen.

Did anyone remember Yolanda's birthday cake, laced or should I say drowned in Barbados rum? Unlikely, but they could probably remember the hang-over better!

Some of them were straight-A students, and some of them weren't. I will leave you to guess which Sarah was.

They discussed Reading Pop Festival and Sarah remembers seeing Rod Stewart on the main stage and playing Spot the policemen. They had hippy clothes but highly polished shoes (the policemen not Rod Stewart).

They are looking forward to another time together next week.

She then had a lovely phone call with her friend Maggie.

I thought Sarah's ears might drop off; she did have to put in a new hearing aid battery, I guess she had worn it out.

# 20TH JUNE

I considered myself very well behaved over the last few days. Sarah's memory is so dodgy that I could say anything and she probably wouldn't be able to dispute it.

I say that because she forgot to say yesterday that I had been in high spirits, and in her words, exceptionally naughty.

It all started when she came down for breakfast, well I would have called it almost lunch time. But then I am on a different timing regime from the old codgers.

She walked into the breakfast room and could hear Celia's scolding voice coming from the kitchen. It's a bit higher pitched than her usual one, so I knew I was in trouble.

'Get out of the breadbin you naughty cat!' She paused to catch her breath, I just *pawsed*, which means the immovable object meets the immovable force.

Celia tries to appeal to my conscience, but I pretend I haven't got one. Celia speaks firmly but kindly, Sarah tries to appeal to my conscience but Sarah knows it's a waste of time.

It's no good trying to reckon with me, I don't listen, well actually I do but I won't respond. I can hardly blame it on my hearing, having boasted that cat's hearing is far superior to peoples.

Well, of course Sarah and Celia are deaf, but as Sarah kindly and firmly pointed out, not daft.

I knew a tussle would ensue. Celia's pleadings, followed by a reprimand, did no good.

By this point Sarah had entered the kitchen and looked like Boadicea the woman warrior - feisty, undefeatable and noble. Sarah googled her and it says she was very tall; the glance of her eye most fierce, her voice harsh. A great mass of the reddest hair fell down to her hips.

Sarah's hair is probably the closest thing she had in common with her, except it is not red, but mostly white. She can be quite formidable at times. I have heard her ranting, and her voice raised, it's not nice.

Marching into the kitchen, she took one look at me with a Boadicea fierce glance in her eye.

'Get out of the bread bin AT ONCE.' Did I move, yes and no: I moved further into the bread bin and flattened myself against the back of it.

Sarah doesn't take no for an answer, and I saw her large hands looming in my direction. I tried pleading, 'but I'm not on the work top,' but my pleas went unheard, perhaps she hadn't got her hearing aids in?

I was grabbed unceremoniously around my middle, and squirming I tried to break free.

I couldn't manage it and she looked me in the eye and said 'You naughty cat,' but I think I could see a glimmer of amusement replacing the fiery glance.

Celia breathed a sigh of relief that they had won the battle, but I'm not a pushover, new battles were on the horizon.

That was just the start to the day.

Sarah says it does make my diary more riveting, when I do something rather than sleep.

I wonder how interesting I can make tomorrow?

# 21st June

Have you ever seen a magician pull a rabbit out of their hat?

Sarah's father always said he would 'give her away with a pound of tea and a white rabbit.'

She and her sister thought it had something to do with tea being an expensive commodity. In China, tea was taxed as a source of revenue.

Antique tea caddies often had a lock so that the servants couldn't steal it.

When her father gave her sister away, he picked up his top hat and produced a tea caddy and the promised half a pound of tea, but miserably no rabbit was available.

Googling the expression revealed a totally different interpretation, and was rather deflating.

Sadly, it doesn't mean that at all, it was a cockney term that meant something was cheap.

Shopkeepers used to do special offers of giving a free gift which was usually a bit naff, to encourage people to buy tea.

So, giving either of his daughters away with a pound of tea wasn't actually very complimentary.

What, you may well ask, has this to do with me?

A dead rabbit magically appeared in the front garden just after lunch.

How it got there no one knows, everyone thought I was in the garden with them, but lying low.

I am not prepared to divulge how it arrived, it wasn't a tiny baby one either, it was more teenager sized.

Dave the detective said it was freshly killed as it hadn't got rigor mortis; he took it away and put it into the woods.

So, the mystery is, did I kill it, or did another of our visiting cats leave it as a gift for our ungrateful crew?

We have lots of cats coming to play these days. Chubby Checker because of his size would be capable of pulling of a stunt like that.

Rosie and Ruby are delicate looking, pretty, and unlikely to have delivered it to the front door, unless they did it as a team.

Welly is a possibility, not to mention Tarka and Silver, and Daisy. Then there's a very attractive grey cat which we call Pebbles and a new black and white cat Domino, who pops in from time to time.

That will keep them guessing: lots of suspects and one dead body. Agatha Christie comes to mind, not because she is a killer cat, but she did write very interesting murder stories.

Her titles included 'Three Blind Mice', 'The Cat Among the Pigeons' and 'Murder in the *Mews*,' so I think she was a cat lover.

This will be Sarah's first murder mystery, if she is clever enough to solve it, which I very much doubt.

It was a bit chilly in the garden, and I am a fair-weather cat in the same way that Sarah is a fair-weather gardener.

The old codgers settled down to watch a comedy film in the evening and raucous laughter rang through the house.

It didn't sound my cup of tea at all.

I think I'd better stop mentioning tea, as Sarah looks a bit deflated by her googling.

# 22nd June

Well, it didn't take Miss Marple or Hercule Poirot to deduce the killer of the mouse that was left in my bedroom, just as Sarah was going to bed.

She was thrilled, well I think that was the look on her face, but I wasn't too certain, as she stomped out into the dark of the garden to rehome the dead mouse.

Sometimes it's hard to tell the difference between a smile and gritted teeth!

Sarah has been drawing again, and has nearly finished another picture of me, but has been having trouble with my white whiskers.

Having watched some videos on Youtube, an order has been placed for a special eraser from the nice man at Amazon.

She did wonder how people make money on there if a £1.86 item is sent by courier, but she says she's not going to worry about that.

She and Celia watched another video on their big screen in the morning and I must say I found it very restful and interesting.

It was a Father's Day service from a local church. The old codgers miss going to be with their friends on Sundays, but the interesting thing about this video was that at the end you could join in and talk to other people who had been watching it too.

Being Father's Day they both felt sad as their Dads had died some years ago. It's a bit in your face on the internet at times like this, but Sarah was very impressed that one company sent an email saying if you are finding it difficult you could be temporarily unsubscribed until it was over. The local church was very supportive of those without fathers which was a welcome and refreshing stance.

It was the talking to people bit that they enjoyed too and had meaningful chats with various people from that church.

I sat all the way through on Celia's lap and kept very still, and just before the chatting finished, I was allowed to wave to the people on the other end of the camera.

This started another lively conversation. I feel I do have that effect on people.

Sunday's cooked lunch was postponed and sandwiches were on the menu, I always mooch about to see if there are any crumbs on the floor and being such a tidy and fastidious cat, I hoover them up with my mouth. Sadly, there aren't many crumbs but I live in hope.

I have heard people talking about lockdown and bubbles, whatever they are. I haven't seen any, so I will have to keep my ear to the ground.

The sun was lovely and as I sunbathed in the garden Sarah planted some geraniums. She really would like to get some more but shielding makes it a bit tricky as she can't go into any shops.

She also planted a cleome, which she grew from seed, I do hope it flowers for Sarah.

Daphne had bought some very tasty pork chops which Sarah cooked, even I licked my lips, but none came my way.

I wasn't too keen when she said she was preparing 'Rats are Chewy' as the vegetable, but she assured me no rats were harmed in its making.

I know, as sure as eggs are eggs, that the sight of a rat would send Sarah into a hysterical panic, she's bad enough with mice and shrews.

I know she has encountered rats before, one of her friends had tame ones and she and Celia looked after them for her, when she went on holiday but to be honest it was Celia who did the caring.

Sarah saw a rat one day in her Dad's garden, running up into the dovecote. She screamed and her dad who had just had steroid injections in his knees, hobbled downstairs wearing just his underpants and a dressing gown to see what she was making such a commotion about.

He said he was sure it was a squirrel and that she must have been mistaken, but Sarah insisted it had a scaly tail and squirrels have fluffy ones, and that at her age she could tell the difference.

He ventured out into the garden in his bare feet and Sarah slammed the back door behind him. Looking up she saw a garden cane making its way across the gravel path, above the top of the hedge, like a gondolier's pole. This was obviously was being used by her father as an improvised walking stick, as he made his way to the dovecote.

'Get me my slippers!' his pain-wracked voice yelled, 'Sarah, bring me my slippers at once.'

Eventually, after a few more loud entreaties, compassion won, and she threw the slippers over the hedge and slammed the door firmly shut again.

Her father was not pleased.

It's nice to remember him on Father's Day.

# 23RD JUNE

I do think Sarah is peculiar.

Why you may well ask? I could come up with a whole list of things, but that may be a bit unfair for both of us and it would take me ages to write the list in the first place so perhaps I should just mention a few of her quirks and idiosyncrasies.

She wanders around the garden with a pair of secateurs in her hand, chopping away at the roses and peonies and anything else that takes her fancy. There seems to be no rhyme nor reason to her vicious attacks on these helpless plants. It's not as if she chops at them to pick the flowers, there are none on the bits she attacks and she continues to pull out plants then put in new ones.

Her phone has gone berserk and she seems unable to answer it if someone rings her.

Tie-dyeing is on her list of things to do this week, if the weather stays hot, and she is searching frantically for her special tablecloth to do it on.

I have no idea what she is rambling on about, time will tell.

Tidiness isn't in her dictionary, well that's what she claims, but Celia is not so sure about that.

Celia immediately went out to the greenhouse and returned with the tablecloth. Why couldn't Sarah see it?

Everyone has their quirks but Sarah says I shouldn't list anyone else's, as they might feel hurt, but we have an understanding.

Even her GP says she is quirky and it seems it's a strength, rather than a diagnosis.

Sarah says the best prescription for her quirkiness is ice cream and ginger beer, but her doctor said they weren't available on the NHS.

My day started very early, Celia and Sarah say they didn't know there were two 5 o'clocks in a day. Their sleeping habits are so different to mine and like many people during lockdown they get up late and go to bed late.

I wouldn't describe Celia as quirky but for some strange reason last night Celia had barricaded my cat flap with the food bin and put my bed on top of it.

She obviously didn't want me to have a night time prowl, or breakfast with Billy cat or any of my friends.

What she didn't know was that my middle name is Houdini and I am a great escapologist.

I like keeping them on their toes, will this become another Agatha Christie red herring I so enjoy?

Sarah says it's a fib about the herring, but I beg to differ. Anyway, Sarah hates fish so she shouldn't pass judgement.

Celia will never know how I escaped, and I don't have any desire to divulge it!

# 24TH JUNE

I felt a bit rejected today when I heard Celia say the old codgers were going out for a jolly in the car. Of course, I wanted to go and not be left behind, but I really don't want to face being stuffed in that wicker box they used to take me to the vets in; and then if I wanted to go for a walk with them, I would had have to wear my harness - and if you remember the old codgers got it on upside down so that the lead went between my back legs. I couldn't go through that again so perhaps staying home to guard the property is a better option after all!

That whole process wouldn't be at all jolly, for me or them, as it's very hot, so perhaps they were considering my feelings after all, but I doubt it!

When they returned, they seemed happy: ice cream had been included in the outing. What a great surprise that was, not! But they said the best thing was being with close friends, even though they couldn't be that close. They waffled on about bubbles which I find fun to pop and chase, but I can't imagine them doing either of those things in the heat, and who was going to blow the bubbles?

Actually, as an asthmatic Sarah is an obvious choice because it's good for your lungs, but I know Celia would want to have a go too.

John and Harriet would probably join in too but would be more inclined if their grandchildren were with them, instead of the old codgers. Also, could Sarah be trusted not to get her camera out? I don't think so.

I happen to know that Sarah has got a bubble wand in her bedroom, why? you may well ask.

She takes it with her when she goes to festivals as everyone loves bubbles and they are a necessity. Many a time she has danced and pranced about while blowing them, or chased them with her camera if someone else is doing the blowing.

She said if she has time after tea, she will blow some bubbles for me, then it would be my chance to leap and frolic to my heart's content, well, until Sarah runs out of puff.

That would mean we could all let off some steam, which is very needed as Sarah has been doing big sums and we all know what that means.

I conserved my energy by sleeping a lot today, so I didn't get into too much mischief. Well only in my dreams. Sarah has been dreaming about toilets again, I think she is worried about going out and there being none open anywhere. There are lots of things to worry about in lockdown, but most of them you can't do anything about. She needs to be like me, laid back, sensible, and relaxed.

I don't know what all the toilet fuss is about I can go anywhere, well almost anywhere, beds are not included, unless they are flower beds.

Sweet dreams, companions.

# 25th June

Goodness me I haven't seen Sarah so uptight and shouty during lockdown, since she dropped something on her foot.

She has been nicely calm and mellow most of the time, but today she excelled herself and became very shouty and uttered more than a few rude words. Most of which are unrepeatable here and it wasn't just the torrent of words, but the volume too.

It was enough to make Celia take her hearing aid out, just to get some respite.

Celia kept coming in and offering cups of tea and biscuits and being kind (she always is) and Sarah was so grumpy she ate one of Dave's lunch box biscuits as well.

She does get like that when she is doing sums but as shopping is limited and Sarah still can't go to the shops, she hasn't had to do as many sums as she did before lockdown. I wonder if other people have saved money too. Petrol spending has been minimal but biscuit spending has increased.

Sarah asked Celia to get nasty biscuits next time she went shopping, but she pointed out that there aren't any nasty biscuits, if there were, they wouldn't sell. I suppose that makes economic sense.

Unfortunately, this outburst of bad behaviour on Sarah's part didn't pass quickly, she did shut up briefly at lunchtime, only to resume her ranting in the afternoon.

She was muttering something about meerkats, and looking at videos about them. Do you think this will encourage Sarah to make a video of me? Mind you, I wouldn't want to wear what the meerkats do, they even wear glasses. I do hope she's not thinking of getting one, after all, I am the number one cat here. There's nothing wrong with my eyesight, as she knows, by the number of dead mice and shrews I give the old codgers as presents. And another thing - they spell the cat part of their name with a k, so I don't think they will be as intellectual as me and don't mention spellchecker, it's Sarah who uses it not me. She seemed very confused.com.

This ghastly scenario seemed to go on forever.

It turned out the meerkats were connected to insurance whatever that is.

The insurance company asked where Celia was born and she said 'In the UK.'

They then asked 'Ok, which part?'

and she said 'all of me,' they do ask a lot of questions. I'm surprised they didn't ask about me, that might help her get a good deal. I think they meant which part of the UK not which part of her body. I was mildly amused.

I was so relieved when Sarah decided to call it a day with the insurance quotes, and reverted to Facebook and playing games on her phone. At times during the day, I had to put my paws over my ears, which is neither comfortable nor pretty, especially when it's so hot.

Sarah and Celia went into an estate agent recently and the nice man in the posh blue suit chatted a bit and then said could he take their details. 'Now, can I have your title?

Sarah never batted an eyelid and replied 'Lady.'

He batted more than his eyelids I can tell you, looking a bit flummoxed he repeated, 'Lady?'

At which point Sarah fell about laughing. 'Only joking! Miss is fine.'

He then asked Celia the same question, 'Title?'

Before Celia could open her mouth, Sarah had said 'Duchess!' and gave him a sweet smile, before collapsing again in fits of laughter.

He probably thought she was mad, but she hoped when he next had to ask someone that question, that a sliver of mischievous joy would remain with him.

I left Sarah laughing hysterically to herself hunched over her laptop. and decided she had made more than enough noise for today.

I quietly slipped up the stairs but I needn't have bothered, she couldn't have heard me above her final outburst, and finding a quiet spot I attempted to sleep.

# 26TH JUNE

Sarah got up in the night and crossing the landing, came upon me, where I was lying underneath the fire extinguisher. I thought if it became as hot as an inferno this was probably the most sensible place to doze. I had stretched to my full length, so I looked enormously long for such a dainty cat.

'Dainty my foot,' I felt sure I heard in a whispered leakage from her mouth. Still at least she was being polite, which was more than could be said for earlier behaviour.

She returned to bed and after a while I slipped onto her quilt and comforted by my presence she quickly went back to sleep. Well that's what I think happened.

An hour or so later she woke with a start, and said 'Gosh I think we might be having an earthquake.'

She was convinced that the bed was moving. She changed position but she still felt aware of a tremor. 'This is going on a long time,' she murmured 'what is the time?' Reaching for her glasses she peered at the clock, '6.17,' and she let out a long sigh.

Laying down again she sensed that the bed was still shaking. A fleeting moment of lucidity entered her sleep befuddled brain and she put her hand down the side of the bed.

Guess what? I appeared as bright and bouncy as a balloon dancing in the breeze.

She wasn't as pleased to see me as I thought she would be.

This wasn't the best start in the day for either of us.

I felt very disappointed and sloped off downstairs with my tail twitching showing my disgust.

To make matters worse someone or something had eaten my treats.

I don't think it was Sarah as she doesn't like fish, if it had been the chicken and cheese ones, she would have been a prime suspect.

'Call in Miss Marple' was what went through my mind. Two mysteries in a week - firstly the dead rabbit and now my treats had been stolen.

The old codgers were up a bit earlier than usual and after yesterday's furore they seemed a little calmer.

Celia gasped when she looked at my basket and all my treats had gone; I always leave a couple in reserve in case I am starving. 'This is suspicious' she said and wisely shook her head as she looked around my bedroom. 'Very suspicious, and someone or some cat has used your litter tray too.'

Yuk, yuk, and double yuk, I was intrigued to know how she knew. 'There are large paw marks in the tray, yours are dainty but this must have been a hulking brute of a cat.' I could hear the cogs whirring in her brain, and in her Miss Marple voice said 'I deduce it was Chubby Checker.'

Well, my flabber has never been so ghasted, not just at the speed of her naming the culprit, but also who she thought it was.

Chubby has been my friend ever since I came here, I wouldn't dream of stealing his treats or food.

Sarah who is more Sherlock Holmes than Miss Marple probably wouldn't have noticed anything was missing. She always manages to save a piece of chocolate for emergencies, but she has some friends, no names mentioned, who could make twelve rock buns and eat the whole lot without sharing any of them. She's a dieter too, the See Food Diet I presume.

Sarah was already at the table with her laptop, I wouldn't say she was eager to get on with sums but it had to be done.

I did notice the biscuits were close to hand, hers.

Actually, she was much calmer than yesterday despite it being the hottest day of the year so far.

After calls back and forth with the fleet manager who laughed at the biscuit situation, he suggested Celia should give Sarah some immediately, which she did.

Eventually the insurance quote was settled, and after a lunch of scrambled eggs on toast their friend Prisca popped in for a socially distanced ice cream and a chat.

Celia kindly bought Sarah a bunch of tulips to thank and compensate her for her efforts.

I disappeared and didn't return until one in the morning and found Miss Marple was still up.

She kindly gave me the rest of my tea which I had missed, and then we both went to bed.

Biscuit consumption is up in the UK since lockdown by three hundred and seventy nine percent, but I don't think it was just Sarah!

# 27TH JUNE

It was very, very hot today, and needless to say, Sarah was hot under the collar, finalising Celia's car insurance and breakdown cover. Sarah thought she would need breakdown cover if it took much longer to sort out.

I don't think 'Rescue my Car' covers biscuits or ice creams for that matter, so it's no good Sarah sitting in the driveway looking forlorn, waiting for them to come.

At least the old codgers have a good supply of biscuits, I did generously suggest that Sarah was welcome to have some of mine, but she wrinkled her nose and frowned. Not a pretty look Sarah, not pretty at all.

I skittered in and out of the house using the front door, which was open all day due to the heat. It's much more civilised than using my cat flap. If I am very cross with the old codgers I go to my cat flap and repeatedly bang on it pretending it is stuck shut. That really annoys them, but now they are aware of my antics they just ignore me and walk away. I stop then, as there's no point wasting energy, showing off to an absent audience.

Sarah didn't even take her laptop into the garden - it was so hot she could have fried an egg on the paving, but she decided the kitchen was a better place. She wanted scrambled eggs anyway and that would have been too messy.

She has just gone into the kitchen to make a cup of tea and noticed that the lid of the biscuit jar isn't on properly. On further inspection, it's a new packet of biscuits and the only way to resolve the problem is to eat one, then it would fit properly.

I told her to get back to writing my diary immediately! Any old excuse and she distracts herself from the job in hand.

We had another ice cream visitor this afternoon, the old codgers are always pleased to see people as it is a rock-solid reason for ice creams.

I could hear them laughing and chatting away between licks of the lollies, not licking themselves, like me.

My tongue nearly got sunburnt as I licked myself, but it did help me keep cool.

The old codgers are either slow learners or stubborn, I keep setting them a good example but they never follow it.

When Sarah picks me up and gives me firm hugs, I am always suspicious and last night was no exception. Straight after playing the Brainiac's quiz on Zoom Celia rushed out of the room and Sarah grabbed me. At least she didn't sing to me or kiss me. On her return Celia had this nasty looking tube, which having raked around in my fur, she then squeezed its contents onto the back of my neck. I'm sure she wouldn't like me to do that to her. I couldn't lick it off either as my tongue isn't that long. Never mind I will get my own back on her, Watch this space.

# 28th June

A thunderstorm was promised, I don't like thunder, it's noisy nasty stuff, Sarah said it's just the angels having their coal delivered. Her mother told her, so it must be true.

Abraham Lincoln said 'if you read it on the internet it must be true.'

I like my journaling to be true too, Celia corrects Sarah if she thinks it's not.

Back to the thunderstorm, well it never came, all that worrying for nothing. Sarah said I shouldn't waste my emotions on things that might not happen.

I won't waste any on not getting fed, Celia is as regular as clockwork.

Fearlessness is like a muscle, the more you exercise it the stronger it grows, so I had better get practising. So, must Sarah.

Does that mean I can bring in more live mice, so she can get lots of practice?

I might dream that it is, but Daphne has returned and she won't take any nonsense.

It was her idea to put me into the room with the mouse last time, but I didn't feel any inclination to kill it, it was a new toy to play with. Perhaps the old codgers should get me some new things to play with.

This is my wish list:

1. A cat home with a scratchpad (Sarah said she can make one out of an old box and she will make it look like a house by drawing on it).
2. A cat senses massager. That sounds lovely, it has a gum massager, a ripple massager, a pressure mat to massage my paws. and a body stroke groomer. (Sarah says, isn't that what Celia and she do anyway, so that would be a waste of money. They say I am pampered enough as it is).
3. An automatic food dispenser - (well, that's Celia, another no no).
4. A cactus scratch tree only £65 (do I think money grows on trees?)
5. A cat scratching DJ deck (I have shown no previous interest in music, why would I now?)
6. A Ziggy Stardust cat cave. (I have a bed already, although I prefer cardboard boxes that I have chewed so they have a very decorative edge).
7. A cat activity brain mover, (They think I am intelligent enough, so that's positive).

I can but dream, plead and cajole them incessantly, but to be honest, I have tried that before and most times they win.

When and if Sarah decorates a box for me, I will get her to take a photo.

I won't hold my breath, as her memory is so bad.

I wonder what Celia and Sarah would put on a wish list? I must keep my ear to the ground and pay more attention when they are talking, mind you they do drivel on at times and I just switch off.

Sarah just informed me that getting my diary published is near the top of her list.

That has cheered me up, think I might go out in the last of the sun, and see what's going on outside.

# 29TH JUNE

I have been whistling down the wind. It has been blowing ferociously and we all know what that means, I am highly excitable and skittish. No rude comments please, like, is that any different to any other day? If you can't spot the signs you must be blind or deaf or both.

Take away Sarah's glasses and hearing aids and you would get the idea.

I love the wind, it makes me rumbustious, dance, and fly.

The old codgers spent quite a lot of time watching the big white screen in the lounge, I go in there quite often, but I never manage to catch the people who live behind the screen.

Sarah remembers looking behind the television for the people who appeared on it, peering through the air vent but no one was ever there, and she was only 27!

That's a fib, I must confess, she was probably about three, and when her mother came into the room she screeched 'Sarah, what are you doing, come out from behind the television at once!' Being a mildly obedient child, she shuffled back into the centre of the room, and her mother continued her tirade, 'You must never go behind the television, your cousin Mary burnt her fingers badly when she stuck her hand into the back of the set.'

Being inquisitive must run in the family. I wonder if Mary gets distracted when googling?

I love it when the wind whistles around me whipping up the branches of the trees and blowing the leaves that are fluttering down. The old codgers went for a walk in the woods yesterday on their way to buy some masks from a lady who lived nearby, and a couple of trees had come down. Perhaps they will get Dave to go with a chainsaw to cut some up for the fire.

I thought when they said they were going to get some masks that it would be a Catwoman or a Bart Simpson one, but they returned with limp pieces of cloth and elastic. Nice patterns on the fabric and Sarah, of course, had a purple one and the lady gave them a demonstration on how to fit them.

Sarah offered to buy Celia one from the nice man at Amazon that was black with white whiskers, but she refused the offer. I think Sarah thought we might get confused and although I'm not really a lap cat, it would be a shame if Celia sat on anyone's lap.

Enough frivolity for today, I am just off to do battle with the wind and pirouette about the garden to my heart's content.

# 30TH JUNE

Celia is full of information since she has had a smartphone, she has been telling me how some people live permanently in hotels, or onboard a cruise ship, get everything done for them, all meals provided, never need to make your bed, and have staff to wait on you. No point me considering it, I would probably get seasick, and anyway, it sounds just like here.

I know which side my bread is buttered – both!

It was another fiercely windy day, so two days on the trot I was as high as a kite. Talking of high, Sarah wondered if I was intoxicated on catnip?

I do feel they sometimes judge me wrongly. There isn't any catnip growing in our garden, if I have a secret supplier, I would keep that sort of information under my hat if I wore one.

I did leap onto the top of the breadbin again this morning. Celia can't reach me there but Sarah has got arms like an orangutan and grabbed me and pulled me out, shame really, I do like annoying them if I get the opportunity.

I think Celia has given up on collars for the time being, for me, not her, it was getting a bit expensive having to replace them every few days.

Yesterday Sarah got side-tracked, how unusual, and ended up watching a documentary about a magician called Randi who could escape from a straitjacket whilst swinging upside down on a rope. Impressive, pity I missed it, I might have learnt some new tricks, but I seem to be pretty good at escaping from my collars. I am sure she will get distracted again and then probably forget that she has seen the documentary already.

She says the plus side of her memory loss is that she can watch a film and see it again a few days later and only remember a couple of things about it, which are usually inconsequential fripperies.

I was exceptionally pleased with myself when I managed to get into Dave and Daphne's room today, not once, but twice. This Randi chap in the video seemed able to do all sorts of things, I wonder if he could explain how I mysteriously got in there. Their rooms are out of bounds to me, but I am going to keep them guessing. Sarah wondered if I was now big enough to open the door by lunging at the handle.

One of the big questions of the day was about cat insurance and was nearly as infuriating as sorting out the car insurance. No decision has been made – yet. I will keep you updated.

Sarah has been spectacularly forgetful and seemed very down yesterday afternoon. She suddenly announced mid-afternoon that she was going to her bedroom to watch a film.

Of course, today she can't remember what it was that she watched.

She said she started a couple of films and realised Celia would really enjoy them, so went onto another one, so she could watch it with her.

One of them was called 'Toast' and was an autobiographical account of Nigel Slater the food writer. 'That sounds an interesting job,' said Sarah our gourmand, her eyebrows rising with joy and delight, 'mmm, two things I like, rolled into one, eating and writing.' I will have to keep an eye on her I don't want her to get side-tracked and not complete writing about me.

She can be very fickle.

# July 2020

Don't put all your eggs in one basket, not if I am around.

# 1st July

Sarah had an outing, the first time she had been near a shop since March.

She has been blathering on for ages about wanting to get some geraniums.

Off she popped to Morrison's wearing her new purple mask.

She had chosen there, because their plants are outside the main store and that meant Daphne could go and pay for them, after queueing at the till. After a fair amount of rootling about and going through the boxes of plants, a suitable selection was made and Sarah handed over the money and then sat in the sun keeping a strict distance from everyone else. Daphne drew the short straw and waited patiently in the socially distancing queue.

It reminded Sarah of going to her Dad's with her friend Lynne, and how they went plant buying the day before he opened his garden for charity. Lynne said the return journey was like travelling in a hearse, she had never seen so many plants in a car before. Of course, then they all had to be planted before the sun went down, it was such a lovely memory. Sarah has a genetic love of gardening and finds it very therapeutic.

She rambles on about her grandparents, she remembers her maternal grandfather, Papa, saying that he grew lilies because her grandmother's name was Lily, and showing her the brass fireman's syringe that he used to water the plants in the greenhouse. However he also grew lots of roses as they were her grandmother's favourite flower. Her paternal grandfather, Grandpa, had very green fingers too and she remembers him growing Melons in a hot box in his garden; his conservatory awash with geraniums and the earthy smell that goes with them.

It's strange how smells carry such nostalgia. For me it's tuna, I remember once popping into someone's garden and they came out with a whole bowl of tuna just for me.

Acts of kindness are never wasted and are valued even more so during lockdown, I am hoping it won't just happen while we are struggling with cabin fever, but that it will become a habit.

My acts of kindness involve being friendly to cats that come into our garden and sharing the space with them. Playing with them too, but doesn't extend as far as inviting them into the house because the old codgers don't approve. They said they didn't want the house overrun with cats or mice and if they are like me, they might bring livestock as gifts. The cats, not Celia and Sarah.

Oh yes, I am kind at home too, and comfort Celia when she needs it, and I let her pour everything out to me. I am always a good listener, and I never answer her back, I just agree with her, which you may have noticed!

I put up with Sarah's photographing my every move. She really is like the paparazzi, very sneaky. She said she wants some lovely photos for my book, although she also said she may use them to do pen and ink drawings instead. I do hope she's good at sketching. I will have to make sure I approve of any pictures of me, I wouldn't like to be portrayed as lazy, grumpy, or unkind, I am sure I will make my feelings known. After all, I do love attacking cardboard boxes and paper, and drawings are on paper if you get my drift.

I am now going to be kind and make Sarah's bed warm where my body curls up on it, but I don't think she will see it as kindness. She is rather short-sighted. Thank goodness for Specsavers.

Sarah benefitted from three acts of kindness, well probably more than that today: Daphne took her to get her plants, Hilary came over, bearing the gift of homemade ginger ice cream and Sonya surprised her by popping into the garden with a large bouquet of flowers. She said she could read between the lines in Sarah's writing and thought she needed cheering up.

How wonderful to have such lovely friends.

I wonder if Chubby Checker will turn up with something for me, a half-chewed mouse perhaps or the remains of a partly eaten packet of treats?

# 2ND JULY

Celia and Sarah had both gone into their bathrooms at the same time this morning and I decided to do lot of rolling onto my back, so when they emerged from the bathrooms I was seductively sprawled out and waiting to see which one would be first to rub my belly.

Celia amazingly stuck it out, but Sarah weakened much quicker.

I decided it was a day to look appealing and would practise my skill at every given opportunity.

When Daphne left, Sarah was sitting on the cobbles in the front garden and had just begun weeding. When she returned hours later, she was still there, but the flower bed was looking much better. In fact, she was still sitting on the cobbles and admiring her handiwork and looked in a better frame of mind.

I mooched around and walked exactly where she had just planted, and I can assure you her face wasn't a wreath of smiles then. In fact, it looked decidedly scary, I tried lying on my back and looking appealing, but Sarah was not impressed. She intimated that Marilyn Monroe who I was trying to imitate, however attractive, wouldn't have laid in a flower bed. I don't know how she knows that, but I guess she will have googled something like 'Marilyn Monroe in a flower bed.'

She had, and there were a lot of photos of her lying on a bed, or quilt covers lying on a bed with her portrait photos printed on them. She also discovered Marilyn was a dog fan and had a Maltese terrier given to her by Frank Sinatra. Her last dog was called Maf, which was short for Mafia Honey.

So, she went down in my estimation and wondered if I should imitate another celebrity.

In her favour, she worked her hardest to get Ella Fitzgerald a gig, as she was banned from performing in the 1950's in Los Angeles. She eventually convinced a venue to host her, as long as she, Monroe, sat in the front row for each of the shows. The ensuing publicity worked well for both of them.

Sarah should be encouraged to by the fact that even though Monroe was one of Hollywood's biggest and most well-known actresses she often found it difficult to memorise her lines. Once it took her more than sixty tries to remember the line 'It's me, sugar,' from Some Like it Hot.

That must have encouraged the old codger.

Gina Lollobrigida may be my next star she is listed on Pinterest as a cat lover and there are wonderful photos of her cats. I wonder what their names were, they were just as worthy to be named as she was. The photo headings just say her name, Italian actress, portrait, with cat.

With cat!

# 3RD JULY

Have you ever had one of those days?

Sarah has been muttering around the house going, 'It's just one of those days.'

It started early, when having crept into her room in the night I woke her up, because I wanted to use my litter tray and go exploring. She had no idea that there were two 5.45's in a day and she staggered downstairs muttering to herself, as she went through the house opening all the doors, so that I could roam free.

I followed her down, but when she had gone back to bed I crept back upstairs and woke Celia too, as it's normally her that does that task for me. It makes me feel quite regal, the door being opened for me and then ushering me through. Celia dutifully got up and coming downstairs she wondered why all the doors were open, she knew she had shut them when she went to bed.

It's just that I am a cat of regular habits, and I like people to perform their usual tasks and not employ an understudy.

When Sarah's alarm went off it was earlier than usual, well to be honest she doesn't use her alarm clock very often. She did all her usual ablutions, paying particular attention to her hair, ('about time too' some would say). I wondered why, but I heard her scurrying around, then I heard her say 'this morning I am doing my first proper Zoom meeting as the official speaker for a Women's Institute'.

She was a bit careful about what she wore, she didn't want to get caught out like many people had during lockdown: on conference calls and online meetings where they had put on a shirt and tie or a pretty blouse not realising that their pyjama bottoms, or worse boxer shorts and hairy legs were on display to all and sundry. Sarah hasn't got hairy legs and she says that is too much information!

Dashing into the kitchen to have her reviving cup of tea and fruit with low-fat yogurt, she grabbed the bag out of the freezer then setting up her laptop she discovered it wouldn't connect to the internet - this was a major disaster for a Zoom meeting then she poured frozen runner beans into her yogurt bowl.

Things weren't going too well.

Instead of looking as cool as a cucumber, a look she has honed over the years, she was now in a bit of an anxious state.

I don't really know what Zoom is, but lots of people seem to be using it and loads of small faces appear on a screen and then begins with a lot of miming by those who haven't unmuted their speaker and a lot of shouting by those who have, accompanied by wild gesticulations.

Time is short on Zoom and Sarah only managed to read one story from her book, The Memory Box, and had no time to read anything by me. People asked where I was, which was nice, but I had disappeared out of Sarah's way, so they had to do with a photo instead.

Her laptop seemed to have taken on a new life of its own, she blamed it on the previous night's Windows 10 upgrade. She tried to sort the problem out herself, googling about the update and how to reconnect to the Wi-Fi, as it would be very inconvenient without it, but eventually she had exhausted all her options, as well as herself.

I heard a strangled cry from the breakfast room, and so did Celia who was clutching a book that had just been delivered by the nice man from Amazon. Armed with the wise words of 'The Boy, the Mole, the Fox and the Horse,' she quoted: 'What is the bravest thing you ever said?' asked the boy. 'Help,' said the horse. 'Well Sarah I think you should ring John and see if he can help you.' I agreed, her short temperedness and rude words were bubbling beneath the surface but only just, so I went and lay on her bed, which I felt was more beneficial under the circumstances.

John was very helpful, despite Sarah's incompetence to explain what was wrong. This online help was hindered by her inability to point the camera on her phone at her laptop screen so John could guide her. Poor John, he was very patient and went through lots of variables to attempt to correct the problem.

Sarah calls John 'Mr Magic Fingers' because usually she comes and says something isn't working and then he does the same thing and it works, making Sarah feel silly, but this time, perhaps his fingers being remote it didn't work at the first attempt.

Eventually, once back online, the phone call came to an end and John could breathe a sigh of relief, and so could Sarah, until she went to watch Paddington 2 on the big screen in the lounge.

After a delicious meal cooked by Daphne, Sarah suggested a film night, and everyone agreed it was a good idea.

There was no sound, well apart from Sarah saying for the umpteenth time, 'it's just one of those days.' Her laptop was now silent, and no matter what she did, it wouldn't speak.

In the end, after looking at the settings and faffing about, Dave brought in his speakers and that worked, so their evening's entertainment went ahead.

Once uncoupled from the projector the volume came back, Sarah sighed and returned to posting yesterday's diary entry, inadvertently missing out the photos of me, a big mistake!

Then she went to bed, glad that tomorrow would be a new day.

# 4TH JULY

Sarah spent most of yesterday tapping away at her laptop, and she said today's diary entry will be shorter, as she has other things she wants to do. I think that's a bit selfish of her, but I mustn't complain, or she may decide she doesn't want to write about a whinging cat.

I could have her up for defamation of character, but the best thing to do is operate a charm offensive, which is defined in the dictionary as a campaign of flattery, friendliness, and cajolement designed to achieve the support or agreement of others.

Sneaky eh?

I will for the time being be amenable, friendly, and kind. I will let Celia brush my coat without complaining, attempt to overcome my taste for cardboard boxes and not chew Sarah's letters.

Celia said I need to include not sitting on the breakfast room table, not bringing in live animals or looking at her legs in a menacing way.

Sarah would add, running off when she wants to take my photo, or closing my eyes at the wrong moment. Photos of black cats are much better with their eyes open, otherwise they could look like a black blob. I consider that a very rude comment and I feel quite offended when she says I am difficult to draw. She even said, 'If you were a lighter coloured cat it would be so much easier.'

I suppose she would only have to draw the outline which would be much quicker, but I like her to have a challenge to rise to.

She is still looking at publishers and would like to have my diary in the shops and online for Christmas. She could do mugs and t-shirts too! I think she may be getting a bit carried away, but she says you must dream big.

C.S. Lewis says, 'You are never too old to set another goal or to dream a new dream.'

# 5TH JULY

Sarah really is the limit and has no idea what privacy means. I told you yesterday what a pain she is with her camera, the paparazzi have nothing on her. Fancy taking a picture of me having a wee!

I said 'is nothing sacred?' and would you believe it, she said 'if you persist in weeing and digging holes in my flower bed you should be grateful that it's only a camera that I'm shooting with!'

I presume she was implying that she had a catapult. I'm not sure exactly what a catapult is but I think it might have something to do with cats flying. I don't mean on a plane either, some cats are very agile and give the impression that they can fly by doing death defying leaps from one place to another. I am a bit shy so she won't get any pictures of me flying, but then I said that about using the flower bed as a giant outdoor litter tray.

Even now her camera is on the table in case I do anything newsworthy.

Yesterday had a newsworthy event. Celia came out into the garden and started weeding between the cobble stones. She said she couldn't do it wrong and had been inspired by Daphne setting the example.

I of course, decided I should get in on the act, and after patting a fallen apricot from the tree by the vine, I got down to business.

The cobbled pathway to the kitchen door is looking much better, but the hedge by the door isn't. It looks a bit like Sarah's hair does today - bits sticking up everywhere. Whoever invented the saying 'A bad hair day' must have been inspired by her or at the very least had her in mind.

I didn't actually pull out any weeds, but I supervised Celia and I think she was very grateful.

Sarah was putting in more plants, I must admit it will look nice when they all are in flower, but she is making it really difficult for me to 'get down to doing my business' as the gaps between the plants are getting smaller and she deliberately plants something if she notices the indentation I have left in the soil.

I'm sure she would consider it a great intrusion if I came into the bathroom when she was using it. So far, I haven't subjected her to such an indignity, but I do sometimes hang around outside the bathrooms in an effort to trip her up as she comes out.

Celia had fish and chips for lunch, but she didn't offer me any, she just kept licking her lips.

In the evening Sarah continued with a drawing she has made of me, the one that reminds her of Judi Dench. She said it's something to do with my eyes, mind you in another of her attempts she said my eyes reminded her of her dad. I can't see any similarity at all but perhaps if I had met them, I would be more discerning. Sarah hasn't met Judi Dench, I wouldn't like you to think she was namedropping, but she has enjoyed seeing her in films. Sarah has met her own father, but he died some years ago, so I will have to make do with comparing myself to his photos.

She has been having problems with whiskers, Sarah not Judi Dench, she says it's very hard to draw white whiskers especially on a black cat. I couldn't see the problem myself but then to be honest I would have thought drawing white whiskers on a white cat would be much harder.

I will point her in the direction of YouTube, and see if anyone there can give her some assistance.

I'm not sure what photograph of me she is planning to use, but my solicitor will be in touch if it's an invasion of privacy.

# 6th July

I know I shouldn't brag about it, but Sarah seems to have lost the photo of me having a wee on her precious flower bed!

Just because she saw me do it, she thinks she has recorded it.

Before she had a stroke, her visualising ability was par to none. If she was looking for something, she could recall the last place she had it, mentally, and almost every time she found what she was looking for.

Her boss used to say that Sarah worked by the volcano method. Her desk would be overflowing with piles of papers, but if she asked her for something particular, miraculously, she would find it straight away.

Sadly, it's not the same now, she still lives in volcano mode with papers and clothes and books in piles (and very precarious ones at that), but she has no idea where things are and relies on a mixture of prayer and Celia's intervention to locate all types of things. Of course, I love going into her bedroom and causing havoc, I tiptoe about and leap like a gazelle from pile to pile. Which brings me neatly back to flying cats.

I knew it would be dangerous to suggest Sarah looked on You Tube, I knew it wouldn't just be drawing cats that would catch her eye. She quickly went from drawing cats, to flying cats, then to Cute and Funny Cat Videos to Keep You Smiling, to Cutest Meows Ever, then to America's Got Talent and it was downhill all the way from there. She insists you can learn some amazing facts on You Tube, as I am sure you can imagine.

Lockdown must have attracted millions of people to take part in its fount of all wisdom. How to Cut Your Own Hair, How to Bathe a Nervous Cat. How to Trace Your Family Tree. Well did you know that the ferocious 'Highland Tiger' from Scotland is more endangered than its Asian cousin? I didn't, but Hamish is very popular with lady cats and very good at looking after his kittens. Bully for him!

Celia has been watching videos on people who are deaf, hearing for the first time and people who were colour blind, discovering the beauty of our multi coloured world, with special glasses.

As you can tell she is a bit more discerning than Sarah, well that's what she would like you to think, so I won't spoil the illusion.

Sarah has found that the stroke has damaged her executive functioning skills, which includes following instructions (like recipes), starting tasks and staying focused, keeping track of what she is doing, forgetting what she has just heard or read, keeping track of her belongings and managing time.

She has developed new ways of doing things, she 'cooks by kindle light,' watching a video of someone like Mary Berry and being able to replay it going backwards and forwards has improved her cooking no end. She still tends to forget it's on the stove, so alarms are very necessary, but frequently forgets to set them which doesn't help!

Having to give up driving was a serious blow, but she kept losing the car and forgetting where she was, as well as her reactions being slower. She had to think about other road users and pedestrians, not to mention passengers, who must have been terrified as she would suddenly shout, 'Where are we, where are we?' It was a relief to all when Sarah hung up her car keys.

She got inspired by the saying 'Don't Curse the Darkness – Light a Candle' and with that mantra, she makes the best of what she's got left!

I count my blessings that Celia is responsible for feeding me.

# 7th July

If we had a dog house Sarah would definitely be in it this morning!

Dave and Daphne had planned a well-deserved lie in, and Celia and Sarah had no need to get up early either, or so they thought.

What Sarah had omitted to tell anyone and of course had forgotten herself, was that a man was coming to test the smoke detectors. She had written it in the diary but the page hadn't been turned so no one else knew.

It was what you would call a rude awakening, more than rude in my opinion, obscene would be a better word. Celia banged on Sarah's door and informed her what was about to happen, so she didn't rush out of the house half-dressed and panicking that the house was on fire. Mind you I would have liked to see that, not the half-dressed bit but Sarah hotfooting it, hair unbrushed and in a mild stupor.

We certainly need smoke detectors with Sarah's cooking, when they go off, it usually signifies dinner is ready. Her friend Hugh is very gracious and usually says 'It's not burnt, it's caramelised.'

A burnt offering more like!

Celia tried to get me into the garden as she knew what was about to happen, but of course I always want to do what I want to do, and today was no exception. I was just walking through the breakfast room when the alarm went off. I nearly leapt out of my fur. Of course, I had heard it before, what with Sarah carbonising food - she refers to it as cooking, but I had forgotten how penetrating it is. All the alarms are linked in the house and all go off at the same time.

I bet all the neighbours are thinking,' Gosh Sarah doesn't normally set the alarms off in the mornings' and then surprises everyone.

I like surprises, and I love leaving the old codgers surprises too, but they still don't appreciate them.

I wondered if it was because they would have to share it, so this morning I left them two presents.

Sarah says the best way to get an equal share is to let one person cut it and the other person choose.

It works especially well with cake and children. Not that I advocate halving a child, what I am trying to say is that children learn how to divide things very exactly when the other person is choosing.

Mice might be a bit more difficult, so Sarah says she would let Celia have first pick.

Incessant ringing in my ears eventually drove me into the garden and Celia had that 'I told you so, I did try and warn you,' look on her face. Duly chastened, I made a quick exit over the wall to find somewhere more peaceful.

When I thought it was safe to return, I gingerly stuck my head into the garden. All seemed peaceful, so I presumed the nasty smoke detector man had gone. I must say I did revise my judgement of him as he loved cats, and said his little girl would be really jealous, because she desperately wanted a cat but his wife had an allergy to them. He stroked me very nicely but I do hope he doesn't come again soon.

When he had gone Sarah put her hearing aids in, which was a relief as she kept mistaking what Celia said to her.

While all this was going on Sarah started sketching a portrait of me, this time she said the eyes looked like mine which was a great relief.

Sarah and Celia's friend Lesley came over today and they chatted for ages, nothing new there then.

After she had gone Sarah returned to the sketch pad and faffed about until tea time, when she reached the gastronomic height of cooking tinned hotdogs and onions.

What are hot dogs, they don't sound very pleasant?

I asked the old codgers why hot dogs are the best dogs?

Sarah said it's because they feed the hand that bites them!

Boom, Boom!

She then added that she asked her dad why he called her sister Rose.

'Because roses are your mother's favourite things'

She replied, 'Thanks Dad.'

He replied 'No problem Hotdog.'

I think she might be on a roll, so I am going off in search of better company.

# 8TH JULY

I am afraid I was a bit big headed after I saw the finished drawing of me, I am such a beautiful cat, Celia tells me that all the time but Sarah is a bit more reserved with her adulation.

Sarah spent all day convinced it was Wednesday, I tried to tell her, but you know what she's like, even with her hearing aids in she didn't listen.

I was impressed that she has finished the sketch, she puts her improved skill at drawing down to the Women's Institute. Once a month a small group from the East Hunsbury WI get together and Viv has been patiently teaching and encouraging them. Sarah loves being a member of such a wonderful organisation, and has made loads of friends there.

The drawings for my book are far superior to the ones in Sarah's first book, 'The Memory Box,' - mind you her drawing of the custard cream was passable, but the content of my book is far more interesting. Namely it's about me!

Her first book is a collection of short stories. I can't remember if I have told you this, (and neither can Sarah!) but she finds reading difficult due to her short-term memory problem. However short stories can be read in one go, and she finds them much more satisfying.

Sarah says pride goes before a fall, so I had better be careful what I do today.

There has been a lot of talk about bubbles recently, so Sarah decided to show me what they are.

I didn't appreciate all these strange things floating about. It was bad enough in the garden, but inside the house is worse. Sarah thought I would enjoy playing with them, but I had to take refuge on the stairs, because the bannisters gave the impression of prison bars. Of course, it was Sarah who needs to be behind bars, so from my vantage point I managed to create that effect.

She said it was a shame I didn't like them, as she thought they would be more fun than trying to catch the shower cord in the bathroom.

She may be right but I think smaller bubbles should be first and not the giant ones she blows with her bubble wand. Sarah loves bubbles and wishes she had got a smaller bottle but she felt a bit silly asking anyone who was going shopping to buy her some. I suggested the nice man from Amazon.

He has just popped by and given Sarah a parcel, she opened it up straight away and it is book-mailers so she can post out signed copies of her book.

She has sold a couple of copies this week which the nice man at Amazon sorts out for her, but of course they weren't signed ones.

She said she is going to get me to do a paw print, so that my book has my own seal of approval on it.

I must let you into a secret, my paw writing is, well, fairly indecipherable, that's why I dictate my diary to Sarah and she types it, so anyone can read it.

She thought it would be nice to do a braille version of my book, she has big dreams.

Having said that she is now going to do some research on Google, whoever he is, I wonder how long it will be before she gets distracted and ends up watching videos totally unrelated to the task in hand.

Ten minutes? Five minutes? Three seconds is probably much more accurate.

I do know she has been watching Talking Heads by Alan Bennett and that she frequently reads my diary to Celia in his inimitable voice.

She doesn't mean to, it just happens.

# 9th July

I'm not sure if I have told you this before, anyway Sarah says it's worth repeating, when I was in foster care with my amazing foster mum Clare, she named me Mary. An unusual name for a cat, in my opinion, (of which, as I am sure you have noticed, I have many), but Celia wanted to know why Mary?

Was it because I sing beautifully like Mary Isobel Catherine Bernadette O'Brien, better known as Dusty Springfield, a well-documented cat lover?

Or that I am a great fashionista like Mary Quant?

Do I carry myself regally like Mary Queen of Scots?

I guess the answer to all of these questions, although I think I am regal, fashion conscious and a great singer, is still no.

The reason Clare called me Mary, was because I am so contrary!

Today I certainly lived up to that. I would wail piteously by the front door, until it could be stood no longer and as soon as the door was opened, I would turn my back on it and refuse to go through.

I would then dither on the threshold while the door was held open, so that I could decide whether I wanted to go out or stay in. It was cold and wet and windy outside and no one wanted to stand there shivering like a wet cat pulled out of a swimming pool, while I procrastinated.

If I am very cross, I annoy the old codgers by hitting my cat flap continuously, as if it was broken and I couldn't get out, but they have seen through that ruse, they just walk away ignoring me.

I absolutely amazed Sarah by coming and sitting on her lap, when our friends John and Harriet came to collect a birthday present.

I sat very still and acted demurely as they chatted about this and that and Sarah was amazed by this unexpected show of affection.

Of course, I may never repeat the act, so Sarah had better not count her chickens that I will ever sit on her lap again.

I probably will, but I like to keep her guessing.

I didn't want Celia to feel left out, so I hung around and slept on her lap later, to keep her from rushing to bed.

# 10TH JULY

Tra-la-la- la.

What an exciting day I have had, full of high jinks and adventures.

The old codgers were downstairs in time to answer the door to Sarah's friend Gill from the Women's Institute, which was verging on the miraculous! Of course, I knew that she had come to see me really, so I thought I had better be at home too when she arrived, it would be rude not to.

Her smiling face beamed at me as soon as she saw me doing my Gina Lollobrigida impression on the stairs. I have gone off Marilyn Monroe since I found out that she was a dog lover, but Gina is another kettle of fish! Of course, in finding out about her, Sarah got wildly side-tracked on Pinterest and found lots of famous people who loved cats: Ringo Starr, John and Jacqueline Kennedy, Audrey Hepburn, Picasso, Helena Bonham Carter… the list is endless, but I have reminded her to get on with the job in hand, writing about me, which in my opinion is much more important.

Gill is a wonderful fan of mine and she didn't come empty handed either! She brought me presents - some fish shaped catnip treats and a delicious chicken and liver stick which I gobbled in no time.

Celia wondered if it was the catnip that made me as high as a kite but Sarah doesn't think so.

She said I am high spirited by nature, well we will see who is right, because Sarah has just given me some more, so that she can take another photograph of me.

Who on earth would want to see me eating? Well I guess I must trust Sarah's judgement and she says my adoring fans will love it.

I felt sorry for the old codgers because all they had for their evening meal was some leftover spaghetti carbonara from the day before, with a tin of tomatoes thrown in.

I stayed in the whole time Gill was with us as I didn't want to disappoint her by sloping off. I like the old codgers' friends, especially the ones who don't like cats! I always make a bee line for them, in the hopes of converting them with my charm and charisma.

Sarah was busy writing about me in the afternoon and after tea went down into the cellar to photograph the gas meter. Why, you well may ask? She had an email from her supplier and needed to record the numbers on that and the electric meter.

My nosiness overcame me and despite having been told *CATagorically* not to go down there of course I did. Sarah had no idea I was snooping about, exploring boxes, I do love a nice box, and there were a few down there.

Sarah came back up the steps, switched off the light and shut the door. I was a bit surprised when the light went off but I am extremely good at seeing in the dark and continued my exploration. Finally, bored with that and knowing it was nearly my supper time I went up the steps and couldn't go any further.

The old codgers then went into the lounge to watch a programme called 'Marvellous' and were deaf to my cries. It lasted an hour and a half and Celia was very mystified about my absence when she emerged. She thought she heard a noise, but looked into the hall and I wasn't there, so she carried on doing whatever it is she does on her phone.

I in the meantime was famished, frustrated and forgotten. Well, not forgotten exactly, because after waiting up for me to come in from a nocturnal adventure she decided to have another look around the house, just in case I was in and she had overlooked me.

My plaintive cry was ramped up to full volume and fortunately for her she found me.

Half-starved and bewildered, I emerged and came into the light. Sarah says I mustn't exaggerate, but it's hard to convey my predicament and the effect it had on me.

Of course, Celia made a great fuss of me, I think Sarah would have said it was my own fault and that she hoped it would teach me a lesson, but like Sarah I am a slow learner.

She is very forgiving though.

P.S. Helena Bonham Carter says never again need your posterior feel inferior. She wears something called a TellTail. It's a tail that attaches on a beautiful black bow waistband, One size fits all and comes with its very own grooming comb attached.

Wearable tails for humans.

She's my kind of woman, perhaps I could get one for Celia's birthday!

# 11th July

Was it the catnip treats from Gill that made me as frisky as a kipper!

Celia thought it might be, but Sarah still thinks it's high spirits, after all I am a ball of fun.

Anyway, Catnip, according to the blurb on the treat packet, only creates euphoria when it's inhaled. Also, the sedative effects of catnip can really help calm cats down, and reduce the effects of stress, anxiety and depression. I wonder what would happen if I sniff the open box?

Sounds as though Sarah could do with some!

I excelled myself with various antics and frivolities in the morning, and made the old codgers hoot with laughter. Prancing, dancing and leaping about - me not them.

I touched Sarah's toes, which isn't something she can do from a standing position. I do think she should come into the woods with me, but I guess she's not very good at climbing trees.

Probably not much cop at catching mice either, she can't lick her legs, all in all she's a bit of a duffer at cat-based activities. I could have a go at training her but to be honest I think I would be wasting my time, what with her memory problem.

I had the house to myself a lot of the day because the sun was shining and Celia and Sarah went to someone else's garden.

Sarah was wearing a very strange thing on her face, she said it's called a mask and it was *purrple* which is both of our favourite colours. She mutters enough as it is, so something else to make her mumble even more, isn't very welcome.

Off she and Celia went, leaving me on my own again. I don't know, that's not very considerate but I guess the old saying, 'While the cat's away, the mice will play,' rings true except the mice won't get a chance to play because I will be chasing them.

I will also take advantage of a choice of places to sleep. A bit like Goldilocks and the three bears.

I really tricked Sarah in the morning by rushing into the double bedroom. She looked everywhere for me. She was afraid she was losing the plot and so early in the day. High and low she looked and just as she had turned her back on the room, I attacked her feet!

She turned around and I had disappeared again.

Not one to easily give up she hunted for me again, but still I was nowhere to be seen.

As she left the room I pounced again, but this time she saw me as I went back into hiding, in a tiny gap under one of the beds. She would never have found me if she hadn't turned so swiftly.

When they returned from their jolly, I decided I would show them how much I missed them, and brought in a small dead mouse. They weren't overjoyed and it was whisked away and put into the woods.

The old codgers then spent the evening in the lounge, watching a brilliant film about Nigel Slater called Toast.

Helena Bonham- Carter was in it but minus the tail. I guess it would have been a distraction and not suited to her character of Mrs Potter at all.

What a happy trio we made. When it came to bed time, they trotted off to their rooms and I went on my night perambulations around the area.

# 12TH JULY

Some people think I should be renamed Terminator as I have been very active catching things.

Sarah became worried when the hedge under the breakfast room window started to move violently - it's the hedge that looks like Sarah's hair. Bits springing out all over it, totally unruly, and dishevelled and that's after she has brushed it!

Back to the hedge. Out of the corner of her eye she noticed it moving. Wondering if it was an earthquake, in true British stoic fashion, she tried to ignore it and continued writing.

It began writhing and cavorting about and she wondered if there was something wrong with her eyes, or was she hallucinating? Now she couldn't take her eyes off it, when suddenly she had a light bulb moment.

She had seen me marching proudly towards the front door with a grey mouse, body and tail swinging from my mouth rhythmically as I walked.

Putting two and two together and making five, she realised that I - and probably the mouse - had something to do with the gyrating hedge, and she was right, we were playing in the thick of it. Well to be strictly honest I was, the mouse seemed oblivious to the game.

A stern tap on the window caught my attention for a nanosecond, and I chose to ignore it.

You can only amuse yourself for so long with an unwilling playmate, dead or otherwise, so eventually I went off in search of another buddy who would be more responsive.

When I came in through the cat flap Sarah leapt from her chair, to make sure I hadn't invited any friends in, dead or alive.

I wouldn't have dared!

During the day I had been left alone, as the old codgers went to eat cake, whilst socially distancing, in Celia's sister's garden. The sun was shining and the cake was consumed!

They then went on a drive about, and got into the wrong lane, due to Sarah's navigating and forgetting what the sat nav had just said. Despite it being a bit fraught Celia did very well driving her new car.

Returning to the topic of the hedge, Sarah's boss once offered to cut her hair into a topiary style, with his hedge clippers. With that in mind I think Sarah will be trimming the hedge in the next day or two.

Her hair, that's a different matter entirely.

# 13TH JULY

The sun was up very early this morning, well it always is, so I don't know why Sarah is so surprised.

The surprise is that she staggered to the bathroom and looked out of the window, but of course she trotted back to bed to snooze a little longer, or even a big longer in her case.

It's a shame she misses the sunrise, I find it so tranquil, listening to the birds singing and thinking of breakfast. Not that I would eat a bird, I prefer Mice Crispies for breakfast, and anyway Celia dutifully gets up to feed me, even if she too returns to her bed or goes to have a soak in the bath.

Some people think I live the life of Riley, whoever he is? Of course, Sarah had to google the question and to back it up use The Brewer's Dictionary of Phrase and Fable. So much opportunity to get distracted. Riley was a character in an Irish comic song, and it means to live luxuriously. The hero in the song is a man who describes what he would do if he struck it rich. She then flitted past putting lipstick on a pig, then onto literary place names - once she gets going, there's no stopping her.

Fortunately, the weather was much better and everyone sat in the garden, which was a jolly good job as we were inundated by dogs. Well two to be exact.

In the morning Molly came, a spaniel who was as surprised to see me, as I was her. I gave her a cursory glance and let her get on with playing on the lawn with her lovely family.

The afternoon was different and it was hotter and Brian popped by with his mother's dog Sonya. She has a reputation that goes before her – for nipping at Dave's toes once - and she made herself comfy by the pond.

I considered this a great intrusion on my territory, Sarah said that she wouldn't be there long and not to get too fussed by it.

My hackles rose and if you don't know what they, then I am about to educate you. They are the hairs on the back of an animal's neck, which stick up if they are fearful or angry.

My hairs were totally vertical, and Sarah said she had had a couple of incidents like that herself.

One day a rat got into the chapel during a service and scampered across the room. Sarah's fear made the hair on her neck stand on end and on the neck of the person who sat in front of her - he thought she was a bit of a wimp.

I can't imagine why she feels so scared?

# 14th July

Last night I crept upstairs and launched myself onto Sarah's recumbent body as she was trying to get to sleep. She didn't mind, well she didn't say she did, so that's as good as it gets.

Actually, she laughed, and I went and made myself comfortable under a chair in the corner of her room. She did get up in the night and thought I was still under the chair, but I wasn't.

I had spent a lot of the day loitering, chiefly in Sarah's room, as she has got a very luxurious blanket and the sun shines on me.

I kept out of Sarah's way as she was in a very shouty mood. She always gets like that when she is doing sums. One of the good things about lockdown is that not much cash has been spent, but Sarah's credit card has taken rather a hammering with online purchases.

The result has been that Sarah hasn't had to do loads of sums until today, so she set to and made inroads into the household accounts. Sums aren't her best subject, and her temper wasn't at its best either. I could hear the sounds of her shouting and mumbling to herself from upstairs.

Actually, she didn't use too many rude words, well not that I heard, but she may have mumbled some under her breath. I popped down at meal times, as I didn't want to inconvenience Celia in any way.

Sarah has just spotted me trotting towards the house with a mouse between my teeth and is shaking her head in disbelief.

Like all ballerinas, I have to put in plenty of practice and the garden is ideal and catching mice is a bi-product of my graceful manoeuvres. I love to dance like a butterfly, and if I catch one in my mouth that's a bonus.

Sarah doesn't agree, once she was dancing in a field and as she cavorted doing her Julie Andrews impression, mouth opened wide, a butterfly got in the way and she half swallowed it. She managed to grab a bit of it before it made its way to her tummy, is that where the expression having butterflies in your tummy comes from?

Even the Queen of England has butterflies in her tummy when she opens Parliament, so as usual Sarah is in good company.

Sarah has had great difficulty getting a photograph of me dancing, so until she does you will have to make do with an understudy.

# 15TH JULY

Mice are nice, well in my opinion they are. Sarah said the only mice she likes are chocolate ones or pink sugar mice, which she hasn't had since her childhood. Sweet shops have played major parts in her life.

Her grandfather, 'Papa', was a newsagent, tobacconist, confectioners, which is what they were called in those days. Surprisingly she can remember sitting on the flap of the counter, her legs swinging back and forth when she was three or four. Customers coming in would ask her grandfather if they could give her some chocolate. I say surprising as her memory is so bad and it happened in the last century. I just want you to realise how old she is. In cat years Celia is nearly four hundred and ninety!

The smell of the newspapers is evocative and reminds her of lazy afternoons reading her comics, as well as mornings spent in the shop.

Her first Saturday job was in a sweetshop too.

Anyway, I don't catch pink sugar mice so that's hard luck for her, and she has shown only distain for the grey and brown ones that I have given her, although I must admit they don't taste sweet, a bit like rabbit is the closest description. She doesn't like that either, what a fussy eater.

I take after Celia, who eats anything, with the exception of mice, shrews and rabbits and sometimes rice pudding.

She said if eating was an Olympic sport, she would be a gold medallist, so she is a shining example to follow. She doesn't have a weight problem either, unlike Sarah who could just look at a cream cake and put on weight. Trouble is if she sees one, she eats it, well only if it's hers!

Lockdown has been difficult too, with lots of nice biscuits in the jar and Sarah has weakened, not to mention taking an active part in the house's hospitality, where they offer visitors ice cream in the garden and of course it would be rude to offer them some and not take part themselves.

I think they are very selfish, because although I have pointed out the fact that you can get ice cream pops for cats, none have appeared. It's amazing all the things you can buy for cats these days. I will drop a couple of hints about a water fountain along with the ice cream pops but the chances are if it's Sarah treating me, she will choose something boring like tuna flavoured laxative.

She means well.

# 16TH JULY

Sarah noticed that I was in a bit of state today. I really didn't know what to do with myself.

I swung between elation and despair. She was very sympathetic; she knows what that's like and lockdown has made it worse. It's not too bad when the sun is shining but the last few days have been cold and gloomy. Even the heating kicked in a couple of evenings last week.

Sarah and Celia don't like being cold, in fact Sarah has bought an electric fleece to use, as it's economical and you can curl up in it and feel snug. She won't let me on it though, which is rather mean.

Celia who is a bit of a cat whisperer, made a few deductions about my behaviour, and was convinced I was hungry and tired. She is so clever, and intuitive unlike someone else I could mention.

She gave me a bit more breakfast, well it was more like elevensies by the time she appeared! This settled my equilibrium, and I became docile and compliant again, more like my usual self.

I wonder if that's what was wrong with Sarah, perhaps that's why biscuits seem to help her.

Mind you I had some biscuits left in my bowl but I wanted something succulent like duck and venison. Sarah tries to tell me she has cooked my food herself. I'm not fooled - I don't think she could produce such tender meaty pieces in succulent jelly. I know her cooking has improved a bit recently but not that much! Celia buys only the best sachets of cat food, well that's what she tells me, there may be ones I would like even more, but she plays it safe giving me what she knows I will eat.

It has to have vitamins in it too, I don't know what they are but they sound important.

Having been fed, I meandered up the stairs and, seeing Sarah's bed was empty, decided to relax and have a nap on it, after last night's nocturnal adventures, until it was a meal time again.

Sarah rudely interrupted me, she had mislaid one of her hearing aids and having looked in the usual places started to look in the unusual ones.

This entailed rolling her fleece back and cocooning me in the lush softness, but I wasn't impressed at all and worried I might get suffocated. Didn't she know I had been up all night?

I wonder if anyone else names their hearing aids? Her left one is Albert and the right one is Victoria; it certainly confused her doctor when she wanted to take Sarah's temperature with one of those digital thermometers. 'Let me just take out Victoria,' Sarah said, pausing to rake around in her ear and remove the hearing aid. Her poor GP looked astonished.

Victoria wasn't in the bed and just as she decided to manage without her, there lying by the door was the recalcitrant aid.

I do worry about her, Sarah, not Victoria or her GP who describes her as 'quirky.'

I can think of lots of words to describe Sarah, but I will spare her blushes.

# 17TH JULY

Goodness me Sarah has been very shouty today. I have had to spend a lot of the day with my paws over my ears, not just due to the volume but the language!

She spent nearly an hour on the phone in a queue and when she finally got through to a human, after about a minute she got cut off. I ran off at that point.

I thought queues only happened at shops during lockdown, but then what do I know.

I had put up with her muttering as she tapped furiously on her laptop, she's a one finger typist so although the progress was slow, it had an unusual rapidity for her.

I really don't know what she was on about but I did hear her mutter about new curtains and duvet covers.

I wish in this instance that I had the option of taking out hearing aids. I wouldn't call mine silly names, although Euripides and Persephone have a certain ring to them!

After a more restful snooze I came down for a snack and Celia was gardening, pulling out the weeds in the path. As on a previous occasion, I pointed them out to Celia. Sarah seemed in a better frame of mind and tried to get some new photos of me, as well as doing some weeding.

The postman came to the house this morning with quite a few letters, and the nice people from Tesco had sent Celia a free sample of cat food. She said she didn't think she fancied it, so in her usual sacrificial way she said I could have it.

Tea time came and after fantasising about this treat, especially after I heard Celia reading aloud the blurb about it. 'Irresistible, scrumptious, and luxurious.' I thought, well, I will be the best judge of that. Being so contrary, if something is described as irresistible, I will do my best to ignore and resist it.

She put it into my bowl with a flourish, and I looked the other way. Then I walked off into the garden with my tail held high, I removed myself from temptation, which is more than can be said about Celia and Sarah, and Daphne's homemade lemon drizzle cake!

How embarrassing it was when Daphne offered someone a piece and the old codgers looked at each other in the way naughty children acknowledge a dastardly deed, complicit in an act of theft. Except Daphne keeps saying 'Do feel free to eat anything' and they took her at her word, and it must be said that she had very carelessly left the cake on the worktop in the kitchen, in full view.

I am sure I would have done the same if it had been a nice piece of salmon but it wasn't, and anyway I haven't got a sweet tooth.

I ate half of the cat food, but Celia wonders if Aiden's cat from around the corner popped in and finished it off, as she was hanging around looking hopeful.

Another mystery for the old codgers to investigate, although it may have been a red herring!

# 19th July

The sun has got his hat on, shout 'hip hip hooray' and the BBQ is now in operation.

Having said that Sarah didn't manage to take my dictation yesterday, so today we have two days rolled into one. She said she was tired but it was Daphne's birthday so perhaps it was the planning and frivolities, that, and the fact she is having bad nights and finding it hard to sleep.

No stamina I say, I go out on the prowl for hours in the night and have you ever heard me whinge? She could come with me and see what she could catch, but sadly she is too big and too slow, so I won't invite her.

Sometimes there are deer in the woods near us, but of course she has never seen one.

Sarah's night vision is pretty good, she says it's because she has spent many days and nights in her dark room. I wondered what she had done in a dark room - recovering from migraines perhaps, watching films, hiding from Celia?

When I asked her, it was none of those. She said it was developing films and printing black and white photo for magazines and displays. She said she was an exhibitionist. I think she still is!

Local venues have had her photographs exhibited, including libraries, and church buildings.

Now she does book signings of her first book 'The Memory Box' at Literary Festivals and Women's Institute meetings, and sells some of her photos and cards there too.

For all you Narnia fans, you had to enter the darkroom by going through a wardrobe.

That was very exciting if people didn't know about the dark room. One day she came out of the wardrobe when a friend had popped by and was chatting to John in the office and her friend was very surprised, did a double take and stepped back with shock.

It was a well- kept secret, which not many people knew about, but eventually she got a purpose-built dark room in the church's graphics department.

Many a night was whiled away there, she said it helped her turn negatives into positives.

An abandoned goldfinch was brought to our house at teatime on Friday, not for my tea I hasten to add, although it looked very mouth-watering. Celia and Sarah were like cats on a hot tin roof trying to protect it, and of course I popped up all over the place in the garden.

Celia even tried to put me in Sarah's bedroom and shut the door, but I managed to wriggle free and reappeared a minute or two later. The person who had found it had been hand rearing it for the last three days and it was protected in a quality street tin with fresh grass and some worms dug up from the flower beds.

We all breathed a sigh of relief when it was taken back, I wasn't jealous but Sarah did take a huge number of photos and a video clip of it. Will she replace my daily photo with one of it?

Not that I'm feeling insecure or anything.

Other highlights of the days were ice cream and birthday cake and a film and pottering in the garden, although I got into trouble for sitting amongst the snapdragons and snapping the flowers off one of them.

I hid in the bed the best I could, but Sarah spotted my tail protruding and said I was exceedingly bad.

She has turned into a 'snap dragon' but don't tell her I told you so.

# 20th July

Sarah is a bit put out. She says that I didn't make it clear that when I have been out all night that I usually end up sleeping all day. I do try to choose somewhere that's not inconvenient, like her bed or the best armchair. I wouldn't want to get in anyone's way. Sarah wants me to make it clear that she doesn't sleep all day if she has had a bad night. Sometimes she goes for a short nap, and if I was on her bed, she would, without a doubt, turf me off.

Yesterday seemed a very long day, I don't know why but Sarah felt the same. Not that she was complaining, it's one of the effects of lockdown and shielding. I'm glad that people are living at a slower pace. There's more time to pamper and pander to me!

Actually, the weather was lovely and we sat in the garden together, me lying on the edge of the pond; in fact, I climbed down onto the pebbles and lapped at the water. Celia gets most annoyed about that, as I don't drink a lot from my bowl that she lovingly provides, but I will drink it from any old unsavoury place!

Celia and Sarah watched a Zoom service in the morning, it was held in the church where the congregation were socially distancing and all wearing their masks. There were lots of rules and regulations and hoops to jump through before the church could operate at all. Limits for communal worship have to be decided by the size of the building and worshippers in it. The vicar was behind a Perspex shield in the pulpit and was the only one who could take their mask off during the service. They weren't allowed to sing either, as singing spreads germs.

I do wish someone would tell that to Sarah, perhaps then wouldn't sing as much as she does, it hurts my ears and is the quickest way to get me out of the room. The other day she totally embarrassed me by sweeping me up in her arms and singing and dancing in the breakfast room. I'm sure she did it on purpose, it was a very unpleasant experience. She's no Dame Kiri Te Kanawa, more Florence Foster Jenkins, who is well worth listening to if you need cheering up. If Sarah sings when she is sad, it makes her realise that her voice is worse than her problems. There are times when she sounds like a dying walrus and she hates it if she's singing along with the radio and the artist gets the words wrong.

Her dancing isn't much better, she's no Ginger Rogers, just to show how old she is, or Strictly Come Dancing's Darcy Bussell.

So, all in all, a career in entertainment is a no-no.

# 21st July

Even the news readers looked happy today, and have been saying that the Coronavirus vaccine developed by the University of Oxford appears safe and triggers an immune response.

The sun is shining too, which puts everyone in a better frame of mind, even Sarah laughed when I tried out the mini trampoline. She thought it was hilarious, as I kneaded it, like I do with her fleece.

I love fleece and if Sarah puts hers on the floor or leaves it unattended in a chair, I enjoy giving it a quick pummel. I wonder if there are any more cats like me?

Some people say it's a sign of being happy or content because it reminds a cat of the motion and the comforts of nursing, and its mother.

I do it too, to scent-mark my belongings, and I guess the old codgers come into that category; of course, they think they own me, but we all know it's the other way round! I have got soft paw pads, which means I can indicate that some things are mine and it marks out my territory.

Celia and Sarah should feel flattered if I playfully knead them, as I am saying that I really love them.

Dogs are a bit soppy and if their name is called will run over to the person calling them, but we cats can be pretty dismissive.

Of course, I know my name, but I play hard to get, and don't even mention kisses. Yuk, yuk, double yuk.

Sometimes I put out a paw, to let them know I need attention, and of course I am always lying in their way.

The other day I thought Sarah looked rather sad, so I put my paw on her foot, I think she found it very comforting, but if she put her foot on my paw, I wouldn't be very appreciative.

In fact, at the moment I am playing at, and with her feet!

After playing on the trampoline I decided to sit in the washing basket, as you do.

Unsurprisingly she ran and got her camera and took a couple of photos from the landing window just in case I spotted her. She prowled about clicking, and clicking again.

I thought she was very rude when she said to Celia, 'Phoebe is a basket case,' so I peered through the holes in the basket, and tried to look as if I was a cardigan that had been forgotten to be hung on the line.

'Basket case?' whatever next.

# 22nd July

The old codgers seem to have turned into old dodgers, as I have hardly seen them today; of course, there are lots of reasons for that,

1. I may have been asleep a lot, and not seen them in action, you can't see through your eyelids. Well to be honest, cats are superior as they have three eyelids.

2. We may have been in different rooms, Sarah is usually in the breakfast room, where as I favour the lounge or Sarah's bedroom.

3. I may have been so intent upon catching mice, that I was oblivious to anything or anyone else.

4. They may have gone out, very occasionally Sarah gets in the car with Celia and they pop off somewhere, but they never tell me where.

They do like to have their little secrets!

I was late for all my meals which Celia found a cause for concern. I don't know why she worries. I don't worry when she is late for a meal. I certainly don't go through a list of possible reasons as to her non-appearance.

If I did, I would be in a state of constant anxiety and usually the reason is fairly predictable.

Sarah is slightly more worrying with her memory loss, but she has a sat nav on her phone so I don't worry too much. She never goes mousing, but I am sure when shielding is finished, she will return to hunting in Tesco's. She can sniff out a bargain a mile off, and has been known to loiter at the reduced section for a considerable length of time but she has come home with some great trophies. Legs of lamb, salmon, sausages, pork fillets, corn on the cob, mushrooms…the list is endless.

She is more hunter gatherer, and Celia is the home maker.

When it came to tea time Celia pulled out all the stops to find me, she whistled, warbled and shouted, her shout is much more genteel than Sarah's.

I of course never respond to the first call, and rarely to the second.

When it comes to meal times the old codgers have their routines, Sarah always goes to the bathroom and sings her hand washing song before she makes her entry into the room. Celia often says, 'I'm coming, I'm coming,' and then there is still a delay as she sees something that needs doing, which Sarah never notices!

We all have our foibles, but I can have furballs too!

# 23[RD] July

Slowly and by stealth I capture my trophies, but people are so peculiar, and stop me bringing them into the house. So much for hospitality and equality.

No one welcomes my friends into the house, but then with lockdown no one is being welcomed inside at all, so I suppose I can't complain.

Yesterday afternoon Cookie's mother Pat came, and she and the old codgers basked in the sun while I wore myself ragged trying to catch a mouse. Cookie didn't come but her photograph was shown and admired, She, looks very nice, like salted caramel and Oreo's, an interesting combination and I presume that's why she's called Cookie and not that she has a quirky disposition.

There I sat keeping a close eye on the roots of the climbing hydrangea, poking my paw in as far as it would go, almost touching the mouse who was hiding there. I thought it was very inconsiderate of Sarah to stand over me, camera poised to get a photo of me leaping in the air. Of course, I am never going to let her get a photo of me with all legs akimbo in mid-air. She says that candid photography is using the same stealth as I have at catching mice, and the art of it is to catch the subject unawares.

I think I will have to be more alert.

She was very alert though when she spotted me inviting a mouse into the house. She rushed in and grabbed the dustpan and brush and tried to get us both out in one fell swoop. She missed - I wonder if she heard both of us laughing; she was then heard uttering some very rude words as she tried to evict us.

Sadly, finally she won and we were turfed back out into the garden ignominiously, with our tails between our legs.

Not for long though: after the mouse had given up the fight, I discovered a shrew which seemed very keen to play and so my enjoyment continued until, exhausted, I flopped onto a chair.

Celia wondered if it's the catnip treats that have me so hyperactive, Sarah doesn't think so and I have a feeling she may run a clinical trial.

Daphne did comment that I looked stoned the other day when I came in, but thought perhaps I was just tired.

If the catnip treats do give me an energy boost, I might give a couple to Sarah and see what the effect is on her. Perhaps if I dropped one into her mouth when she is sleeping, she would be able to get up earlier and be more invigorated. Time will tell.

Sarah's mother learnt Latin at school and would often look at the grandmother clock in the hall and say, 'Tempus fugit, time flies, indigo fugit, blue flies.'

Sadly, Sarah didn't inherit her mother's linguistic skills; her school report for French said 'Sarah works to the best of her ability – three and a half percent.'

Her parents tackled the teacher, thinking she was being sarcastic, strange to tell, the teacher assured them it wasn't sarcasm it was realism!

Her father pleaded with them not to make her sit her O level French exam, saying that it was a complete waste of rate-payers' money. The school wouldn't back down and Sarah thought the lowest grade possible was F, but she managed to get an F/H, her dad said it stood for failed horribly!

Her mother was fluent in Hebrew and Sarah only found that out on the last walk she had with her mother before she died. Passing a synagogue Sarah said she would love to know what it said on the wooden door. Her mother Betty just stood there and reeled the whole spiel, without taking a breath. She then translated it into English. Sarah was gob smacked.

Sarah's mother was a very shy person and although she often told the story of her cousin Brian wanting to marry a Jewish girl and how he dragged her along to the Hebrew classes, she had never given any intimation that she had learned anything.

No one ever heard her playing the piano either, which she could, but she was immensely proud of being able to knit since she was four. When she tried to teach Sarah how to knit, she said 'Step one was to take a Valium.' Another disappointment from Sarah then!

Never mind, Sarah has a compassionate nature and is kind to cats, so she can't be too bad.

# 24TH JULY

Did I detect a slight murmur of sarcasm this morning when Sarah said 'I had better write our little darling's diary,' which may have been prompted by her finding me sprawled out on her bed, showing little inclination to move.

I had such a busy day yesterday. I know the catnip treats might have made me a bit speedy, but the old codgers enjoyed watching me play in the garden with them, rather than taking endless photos of me sleeping. Actually, I did enjoy myself, and spent quite a while hiding in Sarah's flower patch, which got her a bit edgy. She has worked hard to make the bed pretty with brightly coloured flowers and doesn't appreciate the fact that I can camouflage myself, in the pursuit of mice.

I didn't pop a treat into Sarah's mouth last night, but I did go and wake Celia up to let me out.

Celia had actually left all the doors open for me, so all I had to do was push the boot room door to get to my cat-flap.

Obviously, I don't suffer with nocturnal weakness - having regaled you with my night time escapades. I can't claim lack of strength to push the door open, especially as I can do it perfectly well during the day.

Celia is a saint, she hasn't got a bad bone in her body, so she dutifully came down and pushed the door open for me. If that had been Sarah, she would have probably feigned sleep, and if convinced that I genuinely needed help, would have made a very theatrical event out of the whole performance. Doing her bowing and doffing her cap impression, or curtsying as she made way for my royal presence. She would have said, 'Who do you think you are the blooming Queen of Sheba?'

I would have smiled sweetly, like the Queen does, when she is waving to people who have lined the street to catch a glimpse of her. Then I would have dismissed her with a flick of my tail as I exited the house, grinning like a Cheshire cat.

# 25TH JULY

Today there was a sense of alarm in the house and it's only a few days before shielding is due to finish. The announcement in the media that Northampton may have to go into a new period of lockdown brought a sense of dread to Sarah. She hasn't been to the shops since March and has a list of things she would like to see first -hand, rather than just looking online.

I decided that I would try very hard to cheer her up, but I needed a nap first!

The old codgers sat in the garden, basking in the morning sunshine. I nearly said early morning sunshine, but their idea of an early morning and mine differ greatly.

Veronica popped by, and they socially distanced in the garden. I saw Sarah going through this strange ritual of putting something in the centre of the cobbled circle by the front door and stepping back and then Veronica stepping forward, picking it up, and stepping back. Then they repeated the action. I have no idea what they were doing but they seemed to know so I guess that's the important thing.

I socially distanced myself until Veronica had gone and then appeared all charm and smiles.

I even sat on Celia's lap, which I don't do very often, but when I do, she is immensely happy and if I could sit still all day, I am sure she wouldn't want to move me.

There was a great flurry of activity in the garden, I hardly knew what to play with first! Mice and shrews seem to have multiplied greatly this week, which is fun for me but not for Sarah.

She rejected my gifts of two shrews and two mice and she then had to remove the dead bodies. She made her way at a funereal pace towards the woods where she laid their bodies to rest.

It didn't even bring a glimmer of a smile; I wonder how many it will take to please her?

On a more cheerful note, Sarah has done a bit of sorting in her bedroom, she says that's different to tidying, but I think she is just trying to con herself into it being a nicer sounding activity.

I await the results, and she has muttered about attacking the cellar, whatever that means?

Time will tell, and so will I.

# 26TH JULY

I found it a bit difficult to tell Sarah what to put in my diary as I spent most of the day asleep.

She thinks I did this on purpose, which of course I didn't.

Something very exciting happened last night though. One of my ardent fans is Wasabi and her human Cris. Sarah decided to video call them. What a great time they had. Cris has had Covid and spent forty days in a small room in isolation with meals left outside her door.

She says that my antics have kept her amused and sane, and if she was the only person who has been helped by my waffling's, I would be more than pleased. Other people and cats say it's helped them too which is great and I know a few people have looked forward to my daily dissertations.

I was roused from my slumber by Celia who scooped me up and helped me to wave to Cris. We both smiled knowingly at each other, grateful that our mutual admiration has kept us going in what is potentially a dark time.

Sarah's favourite saying is 'Don't curse the darkness – light a candle.' I may have mentioned this before but it's always worth repeating. Cris started a Facebook page for cat and animal lovers as a way of reaching out to people, which she has found fulfilling. She's another candle-lighter.

I asked Wasabi if she would like to make a comment on what she has read on Facebook for my book when it comes out, she said she felt honoured. It's good to talk about the book in a positive way, it's never too late to dream dreams.

# 27th July

What a nightmare, poor Daphne awoke at 4.30am and couldn't get back sleep worrying about what the old codgers had done by sending out Birthday invitations by email and Whatsapp.

Celia is going to be seventy next week, and they thought they would have a jolly garden party with cake and ice-cream.

What the old dears had forgotten to take into account was the Covid regulations about numbers.

Having accidently posted the invite on her status it was possible we could have had a huge amount of people turn up. That's the problem with being so popular!

Would you believe it, Daphne had visions of standing at the gate in a police uniform, guiding the unsuspecting throng into the garden. When she blew her whistle, well actually it is Sarah's whistle, lots of people would have to scarper out of the side gate, before anyone realised that more than thirty people had turned up for the jollifications.

She had visions of everyone being arrested as if they were at an illegal rave, not a knees up for the over nineties. Oh, sorry Celia, seventies. Now of course it all depends on two 'whethers'.

Whether there would be a local lockdown in place, and whether the weather was going to be dry and sunny.

Sarah has used the whistle on numerous occasions in similar situations. Her father, a keen gardener, used to open his garden for charity and when it first started there were only three or so gardens that were opening, so on the Friday night before, they all visited each other's gardens and had a celebratory glass of wine at each one.

As the years went on, more people felt inspired to open their gardens and it ended up with seventeen venues, both large and small.

I am sure you can guess what I am going to say, the offer of wine at everyone's home became rather more than could be coped with. In order to manage to get to see all the gardens, Sarah's father had a whistle that he used to blow to call everyone together. The whistle couldn't be ignored, and her father would chivvy everyone to get a move on.

Her father's garden was always the last to be visited and strong coffee was always provided.

By this point many of the gardeners were very merry and it must be questioned how many of them would be able to remember the evening!

Sarah's job, as she didn't drink, was to drive these happily inebriated and many quite elderly horticulturalists home. She remembers walking into her father's lounge where three very tipsy elderly ladies were draped over each other and giggling ferociously. She had quite a struggle to get them into her car, but with perseverance she achieved it and delivered them safely to their respective homes.

Sarah has the whistle on her key ring as a reminder of happy days and nights spent in with her father, and the year after his death, she was the official whistle blower in his stead at the open garden event held in his memory.

The result of all the worrying was, that they checked out the Covid regulations about how many people could meet in a garden and their list would have ended in them being arrested!

Probably not the best way to spend a birthday, in the clink!

The only option was to cancel the garden party and have a low-key celebration at home, so Sarah stepped in and had to contact everyone who they thought had had an invitation and uninvite them!

I watched this drama unfolding before me, and kept a low profile.

Well it was very low, as I pranced into the freezer shed when someone was looking for ice creams and got locked in. Poor Celia wondered where I was. Sarah suggested down the cellar as she was having a clear out, when Celia remembered going into the shed. Fortunately, my plaintive cries were heard and I was welcomed home with great rejoicing.

# 28TH JULY

After the disappointment of cancelling Celia's birthday party, I thought I would try and make up for it. There I was, thinking that perhaps my presents weren't lively enough to be fully appreciated, so I decided to come with a live offering. No pleasing some people, the mouse wasn't welcomed with open arms, or even closed arms.

A note was left on the kitchen worktop to make everyone aware that there was a mouse loose in the house, but by the time Celia had turned up, the mouse was no more. She swept it up and deposited it in some bushes.

Sarah was in a fine mood this morning, not! She was muttering about Broadband whatever that was, and spent ages trying to talk, to TalkTalk. It seemed to be impossible to speak to a human being, and the longer she was kept waiting the crosser she got. When she did eventually speak to someone after four hours of pressing number one for this and number two for that, she was, well how shall I put it, incandescent with rage. I don't think I have ever seen her so cross and shouty, it was much worse than when she is trying to do her sums. She did tell the poor woman on the other end of the phone that she appreciated it wasn't her fault, but all the same it was a poor show - and when she started banging the table while she was talking to her, I decided to make a quick exit.

I don't know what is wrong with her, I am sure she will tell me eventually, but true to form I will be the last to know.

In the end she went for a walk and sat by the river trying to compose herself. I do hope composing herself won't mean I have got to suffer more of her singing, but she wasn't very 'singy' before or after her walk.

The fresh air seemed to have done her some good and she arrived home just in time for tea.

She said she had been watching a solitary leaf being carried along by the current and it had made her feel better. Oh well it takes all sorts to make the world go round.

# 29TH JULY

I love cardboard boxes - they are much more comfortable to sleep in than my bed.

Sarah has been down in the cellar again. She keeps coming out with black bin bags, this is very out of character, so I am a trifle worried. She keeps moving cardboard boxes around too.

The nice man from Amazon has been busy this week, but Sarah is so looking forward to visiting real shops when shielding ends on the 31st. She knows she can't just go mad and be reckless and that she still needs to move with caution, and be vigilant and careful.

The guidance says she can go outside to buy food, to places of worship and for exercise, keeping two metres away from other people, and she has still got to keep washing her hands. I wonder if she will stop singing 'The Owl and the Pussycat?' I 'd like to suggest she sang over the hills and far away.

There have been a lot of conversations about ice-cream this week, I do hope they realise I would rather have a mice-cream, if I am given any choice. I do hope the shops haven't run out.

I have tried not to be irritable or in a bad mewd like someone I know, not mentioning any names of course! I haven't heard her shout or thump the table today so my example must be rubbing off on her a bit. She has a long way to go to match my cheerful disposition and laid- back approach to life.

For those of you who missed me first time around singing the Owl and the Pussy Cat. Perhaps you could suggest something different for Sarah to sing as she washes her hands?

Sarah pointed out that my laid-back approach seems to involve me sleeping on her bed all day, if I get given half a chance. She said she has too much to do, what with taking my dictation and rubbing my tummy, then editing what I have said into something readable, as well as shuffling boxes.

I am worried she may be turning into a sour puss!

# 30TH JULY

After a night on the tiles I crept into the house empty mouthed - no point wasting good mice on ungrateful wretches.

Unusually, Celia was already up and had been shopping with Daphne, almost at the crack of dawn.

Needless to say, Sarah was oblivious to all this activity and when she staggered downstairs there at the foot of them was a huge packet of toilet rolls almost blocking the way. She skirted past it, or should I say trousered past it, and made her way into the kitchen to grab some breakfast.

I kept an eye on her, and when she wasn't looking, I slunk past her and made my way to her bedroom where I knew I could have a sleep with the sun pouring in on me. No wonder she doesn't want to get up. It's almost decadent, luxuriating on her teal coloured fleece, feeling warm and secure.

Downstairs there was a hive of activity as two friends were coming for a meal: a cross between a ploughman's lunch and an afternoon tea. Well the ham, cheese and salad were piled onto a vintage cake stand along with Daphne's fresh home-made bread on the bottom level.

When Linda and Penny arrived, they were very impressed by the banquet spread before them in the garden, and keeping their social distance enjoyed a relaxed little luncheon party.

I don't get that treatment. I can't understand why Celia doesn't go to those lengths with my meals. Perhaps it's a case of familiarity breeding contempt but I know it's not a dislike of me that means Celia fails to pull out all the stops. Anyway, she said there's not much she can do to serve it up any differently, she just puts it in my bowl, while I witter about on the draining board licking the soap or catching drips from the leaking tap. As soon as she puts it on my feeding mat, I am there, scoffing the lot, hardly drawing breath, the taste hardly touching my tonsils. Then I saunter off for a stroll around the garden or search for somewhere to sleep where I won't be disturbed until my next meal.

Of course, Sarah wanted to know if cats really have tonsils or whether I had made it up. She tried peering down my throat when I yawned but couldn't tell whether I had got tonsils or not, so she called upon Google for a definitive answer. I have four, now isn't that an interesting piece of trivia, which may come in useful at a pub quiz. Humans have three pairs.

In the evening Celia picked me up firmly, this always means trouble and probably that something nasty is about to happen. I was right as she then handed me to Sarah who has a firmer grip and produced this pipette with something nasty in it. I wriggled and fought and finally managed to jump out of Sarah's hands, but while I was still in mid-air, she caught me again. I did wonder if she'd ever played cricket? Her reflexes were certainly working well. She then pressed me firmly to her chest and Celia administered the worm treatment before I had time to do anything else.

I really don't know how a spot of stuff on the back of my neck could deal with worms?

The old codgers certainly have some weird ideas, but if it makes them happy to believe that, I will just go along with it. I wouldn't want to rock the boat.

# August 2020

When I am fully charged my eyes go green.

# 1st August

Goodness me I don't know what's wrong with Sarah, it could be the heat, or another underlying cause, I had hoped she would confide in me, she goes quite gooey when I throw myself down in front of her, so I hope she will tell me, but so far, she has kept schtum.

She's not usually secretive.

I think I can read her like a book, but she seems quite inscrutable this week She does keep stroking me tenderly, which although isn't out of character, it's the frequency that is.

She keeps traipsing up and down from the cellar, and has a triumphant look on her face when she emerges into the daylight, clutching a bulging black plastic sack. She even appeared with two sacks, on her final trudge up the stairs. I noticed she had to practically get into the rubbish bin to compact everything down. I was half expecting to see just her legs sticking out.

This is an ominous sign.

Tidying usually means Sarah isn't feeling too well, but she appears in fine fettle, and fairly relaxed. I just don't understand it. Perhaps the thought of shielding ending has generated something within her. Often when she gets into a tidying fit, she gets depressed so I am keeping my fingers and toes crossed. Of course, Sarah had to look up to see if cats do have fingers and toes, and the answer is yes and thumbs too. I could have told her that, but she was insistent that facts need to be corroborated, whatever that means.

She also commented on the fact that the soft squishy pads on my paws are called toe beans.

They are shock absorbers, have a lot of fatty tissue in them which is very helpful when I jump off walls and they also mean I can prowl silently at night, I sweat through them too, but obviously not at night.

Talking of shock absorbers, she did tell me that she had planned to draw a halt to writing this diary when shielding ended as she needs a cut-off point and that seemed a natural place for my book to end. I was shocked I can tell you.

She knows how much my diary means to a lot of people, so for the time being she will continue to keep you amused and enlightened.

I have been a bit bouncier and more playful, for the last couple of days which has greatly appreciated.

I haven't left any gifts, but I may be stockpiling them for Celia's birthday on Wednesday!

Sarah's first trip to the supermarket will be to try and get some ice creams and cakes for the great day.

# 3rd August

I am still trying to get over yesterday's shock revelation that Sarah had intended to finish my diary when shielding came to an end.

Today was the first day of not shielding, but being sensible. Would Sarah manage to contain her excitement? Would she be wise, or overcome with anxiety, as she stepped foot into civilisation and all that the restrictions mean due to Covid?

Needless to say, she is now sitting in the breakfast room, bashing away at the keys on her laptop.

She suddenly sprang into action and was obviously getting ready to confront the world outside the garden. I watched her very carefully, worried that she might forget her mask and then be fined for not having it on. She rifled through her bag checking and double checking that she had got everything she needed.

She set off through the woods with a spring in her step, and a list in her hand.

Her return was triumphant, she had managed to get lots of ice cream lollies for Celia's birthday, plus some reduced bakery items, including a cake. If she runs out of time to cook one for the people who pop in and enjoy greeting Celia on Wednesday, she has one as back-up in the freezer.

It must have been very hard for her to stay in and not go shopping since March, but she has survived with my help. What she would have done with her time if she hadn't got me to keep her occupied, rubbing my tummy, taking dictation, drawing pictures of me, and the vast number of photos of me behaving myself. She's not so sure about the last bit and is convinced that in at least a third of them I am pointing in the wrong direction, pulling a face and you shouldn't take what I say too seriously!

The nice man from Amazon popped by in the afternoon and Sarah got some very jolly, shiny red digital scales. Did you know that milk and water weigh differently? No neither did I but according to Sarah's super-duper scales there is a difference. A gallon of milk is about two ounces heavier than a gallon of water.

I can't see there is much of a difference and anyway why would Sarah need to weigh a gallon of anything? Unless it was melted chocolate, it seems a bit over the top.

My playmates haven't been into the garden much in the last few days, Sarah calls them playmates, I call them friends with emotional attachment.

C. S. Lewis said "Friendship is born at that moment when one person says to another:

'What! You too! I thought I was the only one."

What I thought was so remarkable, was the intelligence that Sarah has, and how she felt a bonding with me.

A stranger walked into my bedroom today, I know I shouldn't mind, but he ripped out the draining board without asking my permission. Where was I going to sit while Celia lovingly prepares my food, and how could I catch the drops of water that dripped from the tap?

Sometimes, I think people forget that I have feelings and how would they like it if I came and did something unasked for in their bedroom I didn't even know him and no one thought to introduce us to each other, a bit of a liberty in my estimation.

Now it has been replaced I can watch Celia much better as I have more room to move about and I don't have to gingerly perch trying to avoid the damp wood.

I hate to admit it, but it does look better.

# 6TH AUGUST

When Sarah sat down to eat her breakfast, I heard her mutter 'Blooming balloons,' or words to that effect.

It was such fun to watch her try and sit on the chair, only to be hindered by a bunch of balloons that had been tied to the back of it, but swung around, so there wasn't room for her bottom to occupy the space!

Balloons you may well as? Well yesterday Celia had something called a birthday which she seemed to enjoy. I thought they had said bath day and I couldn't conceivably imagine what the hoo-ha was all about. She often has a bath so it didn't seem a big deal, except I heard Sarah say a few people were coming around to celebrate it with her. Celia is a very private person so I was surprised that she talked about it so enthusiastically.

Amazingly Sarah and Celia were up first, miracles do happen, which made me realise this was going to be an important day. There on the breakfast room table lay some envelopes and when Celia came into the room. she was carrying an assortment of parcels wrapped in lovely shiny paper and a mountain of envelopes. The post man must have been busy, no wonder he looked tired.

Daphne came downstairs, with presents in her hands too. Talk about a Cheshire cat grin, I thought Celia's face was about to explode with joy.

In fact, the last couple of days Celia has been very excited. Ikea and all its adult playground like settings, was a great pre-birthday outing. Winging her way between kitchentopia and the bedroom bazaar she was overwhelmed with the choice and vibrancy of the lovely things on sale.

Sarah doesn't usually take much notice of furnishings, but at the moment they are both talking about nothing else. It's a bit worrying, what with the arrival of boxes from the nice man, at Amazon. I found one huge box in the dining-room with books in it, which seemed a good opportunity to get rid of some of my frustration by ripping it a bit and then having worn myself out, having a quick snooze in it.

It wasn't from the nice man at Amazon but had some of the books from the shelves in the house. I have no idea what is going on but whatever it is, it's shrouded in mystery.

Returning from Ikea, Celia and Sarah had both bought new kettles. Celia's one was cream and Sarah's was red, she had a matching toaster and they both bought chopping boards.

I have no idea what they are going to chop, but Sarah has a very lethal set of razor-sharp knives which were a present.

Slightly worrying!

I expect you will remember that the old codgers attempted to stage an illegal rave, (I actually have exaggerated that a bit, it was Celia's seventieth birthday party,) but it was accidentally a an illegal size for lockdown. After hastily uninviting people, the day was enjoyable, with a few people popping in and out, and cake and ice cream consumed. Celia felt very loved as people showered her with affection and gifts. The weather was perfect and neighbours and friends enjoyed socially distancing and being together in the front garden. Balloons and bunting decorated the garden from the gate to the front door, and Celia looked lovely in her new blouse.

Sarah accidentally ordered pizzas from Pizza Hut when Celia had asked for Domino's, not much change there then!

She even had a present from Sarah and me, which I felt was *purrfect*, two mugs with me on them. I think I looked very regal.

# 10th August

One of the benefits of lockdown and particularly shielding, has been that there's always someone here to pander to my every beck and call.

Sarah could always be relied upon to be at home except for the NHS clap on a Thursday evening for the first few weeks, and once that stopped, apart for the occasional walk, had become quite a home bird.

Now things are different, and I consider it a poor show that they went to Ikea for hours on Tuesday and showed little interest in me. On Wednesday which was Celia's birthday, she was very pleased with my present of two mugs with my photo on, but I definitely wasn't the centre of her focus.

The other night they went out to look at some furniture, I don't know why, but Sarah has been cutting up pieces of squared paper and rearranging them on an even bigger piece of paper. She does seem a tad grumpy but I guess its sums of a different sort, and as we all know, sums are her bête noire, the black beast, not as threatening as the black dog, but more like a black puppy.

Every time she comes downstairs, she brings a pile of books from her bedroom and puts them into the dining room, Its, all very mystifying, perhaps Celia could shed some light on the subject. I will try and surprise her by sitting on her lap, which I don't do very often and when I have lulled her into a false sense of security I will see if I can get any information from her.

Also, they have spent a long time just talking to people and I have felt very excluded.

Friday, they talked to people all day, I did sit with Pat on the bench for a bit, so I wasn't totally ignored, some people just know how to include cats.

They even went to a BBQ and didn't bring anything back for me.

Poor show, in my opinion.

It got worse, Sunday they went off to look after two dogs, Ziggy and Jazz. That really is an act of treachery. There I was, left alone again, I know they couldn't have taken me but I did feel a bit second fiddle, when I am usually the principle violinist. How unfaithful could they be, Celia did feed me before she went. As soon as she was at home, I heard her whistling for me, but I chose to ignore it. One can only suffer so much rejection.

This taste of her own medicine was of course designed to make her feel terrible, anxious and guilty. It worked I know which buttons to press! If it had been Sarah, she of hard heart and callousness, I expect she would have just gone to bed and said 'Silly cat,' or something similar and wouldn't have lost any sleep worrying about me.

Ziggy tried to ingratiate himself by leaping onto the sofa and licking Sarah's hair, I don't think she was too impressed by that, and what is even worse when he was taken out for a walk wearing a harness, Sarah had to put his poo into a poop bag. How disgusting, at least they don't have to suffer that indignity with me.

I think I have successfully turned Sarah from a dog lover into a cat lover, a feline's friend.

She did say that she might get a cat of her own one day, she would like a kitten so she could train it from the very start.

I don't want to share my love any further than I do already, and I certainly don't want a rival, a sweet, make your eyes go gooey and your heart beat quicker, challenger for the old codger's affection.

# 14th August

Sitting in the garden in the blazing sunshine, a pigeon flew over where the old codgers were having had a little rest from the labours of the day. As they sat there Sarah felt what appeared to be a drop of rain, then another, as there wasn't any appearance of rain, she said she hoped it wasn't an incontinent pigeon. Celia then felt a couple of drops of water on her too and looking up there wasn't a bird in the sky, so they deduced it was rain.

The old codgers went out shopping on Tuesday, they came back with a strange assortment of things, but they did remember me, although I don't feel very grateful for the harness and three collars with bells! They do damage my street cred, but at least they didn't buy me a silly pink one.

I must say I do rather approve of the 'Icycool' tower fan that they bought, it seems very efficient when it comes to lowering the heat and moving the air around.

I think rather a lot of hot air was generated by the old codgers who insisted the McFlurry and Coke were deemed to be medicinal necessities when they reached the half way mark in their expedition. Of course, it started well, when Sarah got out of the car only to discover she had left her mask at home, am I surprised? Answers on a post card please!

Celia was dispatched into B&M where she managed to get three disposable masks for a pound, then the shopping commenced in earnest.

They looked at casseroles and curtains, dish racks and Domestos. Of course, they didn't confess to any of this, I was left to make my own deductions as I peered into the carrier bags that littered the breakfast room, although I thought an aquarium sounded fun.

This week the old codgers have been hospitable. They will do anything to include ice cream in their diet! Wednesday, Clive and his cousin Teresa came for lunch, a long, relaxed affair enjoying each other's company, which involved lots of talking and eating and drinking copious amounts tea and coffee. It was very hot, so I stayed inside sensibly, while they roasted outside and that was in the shade. They said that it's due to lockdown and that visitors can't come inside. Chubby Checker wanted to come in and visit me but he wasn't allowed to, and never has been, lockdown or no lockdown. Needless to say, ice cream was offered and consumed.

Sarah is still messing up her bedroom with lots of boxes and black bags and then storing the ones she wants to keep in the dining room. I must say, I was impressed that she has been getting up earlier this week.

I am still trying to fathom it all out, but I thought I heard her say she has got a flat. A flat what I asked myself? Flat feet? She's had those all her life so I don't see that meriting such a whirlwind of activity. She hasn't got a bicycle so it's not a flat tyre, and spare tyres are the exact opposite of flat, I examined her very thoroughly so I should know.

Time will tell, but I have taken a bite out of one of her boxes to show my displeasure at not being included in the dialogue.

# 18TH AUGUST

It's been very strange here, lots of boxes coming and going, mostly going.

The old codgers have been acting very strangely, and going out every day for hours on end.

I have remained constant in this time.

I brought a frog into my bedroom; one would have thought I could have anything I like as it's my room, but no, not according to 'Bossy Boots'

Celia had noticed that I was in a funny mood, I don't know what she was inferring by that but I thought I was my usual self, although to be fair I wasn't sitting in my usual spot.

I had plonked myself in front of the washing machine looking as if I was standing guard, well, sitting guard actually and thought no one would notice, but of course Celia is a cat whisperer and I hadn't taken that into account.

Taken unawares by a large frog which hopped about in front of them, the old codgers sprang into action.

To be honest, Celia sprung away and Sarah strode in with the mop which Celia had just finished using to clean the floor. I did wonder what she was going to do with it. Sarah stepped back and the damp mop touched her sandaled foot and she thought it was the frog and screamed the house down.

She pulled the fridge freezer forward because by this time I was looking intently behind it, waving a paw in the hopes of catching the frog's attention. It ignored me.

Eventually the old codgers gave up and went back to the breakfast room and sat down.

Some people just don't like a spot of late-night fun.

The dining room is filling up with more books and Sarah has been staggering downstairs with cardboard boxes and dumping them in random piles.

She writes on the boxes but I'm not too good at reading so I only know what she has put if she mutters to herself, 'kitchen or big lounge.'

I did try sleeping on her bed but she was very infuriating and inconsiderate, insisting that it was her bed and she needed to put things on it, and even worse she binge watched 'The Hotel Inspector,' claiming it aided her concentration and made her more focused at the job in hand.

I must admit Alex Polizzi shouting at a hotel owner to get a move on worked wonders on Sarah for at least ten minutes.

I reluctantly gave up as I couldn't get a moments peace, and slipped into the next room and took up my usual position on the pink blanket.

All this boxing and boxes is driving me mad. If I try to get into one, I get shooed away.

Today Sarah was filling one of them up, when I noticed the hole in the side and stuck my paw through it. We did have some fun but then I found out what all these boxes and comings and goings are about. I showed my displeasure by biting the box vigorously.

Celia told me that Sarah is moving, well she does that most of the time, so I couldn't see what the big deal is. She has got a flat a few minutes away and their excursions out have been to start to arrange the furniture.

Of course, the first thing they did when they got there was get the kettle going and make tea and coffee and eat chocolate biscuits.

I still don't know what a flat is but Sarah said I could come and see for myself and that is why they bought a harness. I can't wait to try it on – not!

Celia said it's a lovely flat with floor to ceiling windows, facing south but what am I going to do without Sarah here to rub my tummy and play with me on the stairs.

She isn't moving out straight away but will come backwards and forwards for a couple of weeks so she can get the flat tidy.

She said our house is going to be sold eventually and the flat was a miracle, she hadn't intended to move out now, but Leslie told her about the flat after she had gone there to collect something and thought it was a wonderful place. There are lots of people living where Sarah is going, it's called supported living.

That means I will be left with Celia who adores me, except when I look at her legs, and she thinks I might mistake them for a bannister, or a scratching post.

What will Celia do without Sarah? What will she do instead of tidying up after her?

Will she take up a new craft or skill? Celia not Sarah, who without a doubt has got a few creative ideas up her sleeve.

I will have to be very nice to Celia and she says we can talk to Sarah every day on the portal.

Of course, I am very concerned about who will keep an accurate report of events and will my biography still be written. Sarah says 'it will,' she will get me to update Celia about what and where I have been.

I feel sad, but excited for Sarah, sheltered accommodation to me, means a sturdy bush to hide behind or squeezing myself in the gap above the rubbish bins, a feat that Sarah wouldn't be able attain in a month of Sundays. So, there must be much more to it than what my limited knowledge is aware of. Celia is getting a bungalow, I asked what that meant and Sarah grinning from ear to ear said 'it's a house on one floor and so they bung a low roof on it.'

We will have to see how the next few days pan out I will keep you posted.

# 22ND AUGUST

I feel a little aggrieved, the old codgers have been busy and I feel rather excluded from their shenanigans. Heaven only knows what they have been doing, but it necessitates, being out for hours, depriving me of my liberty. They didn't know I was upstairs luxuriating on Celia's bed when they left, which meant I was stranded from my food and freedom, not to mention the litter tray.

Sarah pointed out it was my own fault, but Celia was much more sympathetic and said the wind must have blown the door shut.

Celia has been seeing relatives, as well as chauffeuring Sarah to her flat.

I wanted to know all about their expeditions, so when Celia looked unoccupied, I took it upon myself to find out a bit more.

One outing started out with a trip to the British Heart Foundation charity shop, as they have a lot of furniture there and they enjoyed rummaging about but came away empty handed.

I absolutely hate the rain, so I was relieved I wasn't with them when the heavens opened and they both got wet. Sarah was the wettest as she had left her jacket in the car, so they scuttled into TK Maxx and had a bit of a mooch upstairs where the kitchen items were on display.

They both have their different ways of shopping, Celia says 'get it while you can, as it might not be available if you come back' and Sarah is a more cautious shopper and always wants to go away and think about it, and needless to say doesn't have a lot of success!

Next stop was a DFS to look at sofas. Sarah wondered why these sofa shops have names like DFS, AFH and ScS. She got terribly confused and wished they has proper names like 'Billy Bloggs Sofa Store' as she was convinced, she had been to DFS already when in fact she hadn't.

It must have been an amusing sight when Sarah sat on a leather sofa and slid off it in a rather ungainly manner. What is it that has made consumers into buyers of furniture in a sludge porridge colour or grey, when all the colours of the rainbow are available?

Like magpies our intrepid shoppers worked their way through the stores and were drawn to vibrancy and 'in your face' hues, they did buy some nice bowls in bright cheery colours and Sarah bought a red Le Creuset dish and would have bought a matching pestle and mortar but they only had it in nude and black.

Who does name these colours?

The whole fiasco wasn't helped in any way by the wearing of masks.

Sarah spent most of her time putting her hearing aids back in after the mask had dislodged them.

This was further hindered by her not being able to hear what people were saying to her, and she became rather fractious and her language slipped a bit into her old Essex vernacular, which has now rather pretentiously been renamed as Estuary English.

You can take the girl out of Essex, but you can't take the Essex out of the girl!

Of course, Celia made a tremendous fuss of me when they came back, consumed with guilt she gave me lots of attention and a nice meal.

Which was more than could be said at McDonalds where they tried two different touch screens to order a McFlurry, only to be told they were out of stock. Never in a month of sundaes did the old codgers expect such a tragic turn of events. Such deprivation taught them how I feel when they go gallivanting off and leave me to starve.

Today the last of the big furniture and boxes have been taken over to Sarah's flat and after a short spell of drinking tea the intrepid shoppers went out again. This time looking for curtains for Sarah's bedroom. Celia is very good at colours and armed with a pillowcase from Sarah's new duvet set they went in search of the perfect match.

But first they went to DFS as Sarah thought she might have found the perfect sofa, only to decide it was the perfect colour but not as comfortable as she had thought. They then started their circuit of the shop, lounging about. I am so glad I wasn't with them, I would have been so embarrassed, especially when Sarah relaxed in a reclining chair but had no idea how to 'unrecline' it. Celia went off looking for a helpful assistant, but a customer said how relaxed Sarah looked. She explained to her that you had to push the foot part with your legs but no matter how hard she tried, it seemed impossible, until she finally got the hang of it. Celia returned to find Sarah on another sofa with an electric recliner and a place to charge up your phone as you sat there. This one was much more comfortable than any of the others, so Dithering Daisy has come home to think about it. The 15- year guarantee was tempting but the colour was bland, grey, with grey flecks in it.

They lost each other in B&Q! Am I surprised? No! Celia had gone on an escapade in search of plugs for the kitchen sink. Sarah rang her but she didn't answer and said she could see Sarah as she was wearing a bright pink top. In the meantime, the target of ten thousand steps a day was almost reached while Sarah continued her search for Celia. They were reunited and made their weary way home. When they came in, I was prowling about like a lion, which probably looked a bit silly, but not as silly as Sarah sliding off the leather settee.

I wouldn't want to tell them, but I think I am better off at home.

# 25TH AUGUST

My meals are still a bit erratic in timing. If I am lucky Celia is there waiting with my meaty morsels, if I'm not lucky, they could be served to me at any old time she feels like it!

I feel rather neglected, Sarah doesn't seem too bothered what time she eats, as long as she gets something.

She seems a little jumpy today, I leapt up beside her just now and she screamed and shot out of her seat, very out of character!

Mind you she and Celia have had a few adventures. The sofa hunt has carried on and back they went to what they call the alphabet shops. Returning to Dfs they went to look at the very comfortable sofa and chair that they sat on the day before. It is in the sale, but it was the colour that was the problem, Silver, Charcoal and Biscuit, or as Sarah said 'Bland, Porridge and Insipid,'

Celia said it was a bargain, which it was if you wanted a pasty coloured sofa, half price, but Sarah remembered her friend Helen telling her about colour prediction when she was studying shoe design. Good old Google. Guess what is the colour for 2021? A.I. Aqua predicted to inspire clarity and focus. Well now you know! Sarah said she would rather wait a year and get a colour she likes if she is spending a lot on furnishings, than spend years regretting a rushed choice.

Homesense sensibly had brighter offerings and the magpies left with six red ramekins and a red and orange pestle and mortar. That bought a smile to their lips.

Csc was another place of adventure, worth a second look but mostly beige and bran colours, with the odd blue sofa thrown in for good measure. A nice place until Sarah tried to get out of the shop.

The automatic doors didn't open, and she was trapped, she could see Celia in the distance, Sensibly in my opinion she had gone to Pets at Home, while Sarah waffled about. She tried tapping on the door, but Celia didn't hear her, she then thought there was an exit next to the doors, so she went to go out of it and slammed her face on the glass. Luckily, she didn't smash her face or the window. That would have made it very exciting. Eventually an assistant came and apologised that they had had to shut off the automatic option, due to lack of staff, and proceeded to prise the doors apart. Celia by now had left a message on Sarah's phone to say she was back at the car.

After that they came home to feed me, about time too.

This moving lark seems fraught with disaster as well as minor triumphs! Today Sarah broke a bookcase, and nearly broke her foot by dropping the futon on it. It's one of those sturdy ones from The Futon Company and weighs a ton and to set it up you need a degree in origami.

It's got a purple cover and was a bargain on Facebook Marketplace. To replace the cover costs £100 so, you can tell its good quality. Actually, it was one of my favourite places to sleep, I wondered where it had gone, along with Sarah's bed. It really is a poor show. I did have a snooze in one of Sarah's boxes, but she noticed me, so I didn't get to see her new home. Celia says she will take me one day with the black harness she bought for me. Dogs and cats are allowed in Sarah's building but they have to be on a lead. Oh, the joy!

Sarah came for tea on Monday and I had meant to play hard to get, but I was so pleased to see her, that I forgot and bounded up to welcome her.

She said she is missing me terribly, but I know my place is to be with Celia who needs me more.

I have noticed a few things since she moved, it must be Sarah who makes all the noise, because the house is as quiet as a *mousealeum*. That's not totally true as Celia has the radio on in the kitchen, at least I am spared Sarah's sweeping me up into her arms and dancing me around the breakfast room. She is quite a good dancer but it would do absolutely nothing for my street cred if anyone found out.

I have waved to her on the portal, it's strange being able to see and hear her, but her body not being here. Her flat is filled with boxes which she keeps moving around, every time Celia pops over they are in a different place. It's a shame I'm not with her, you know how I love boxes but she is bringing some of the empty ones back so they can be used again.

That will be useful if I am a bit cross, as I will have a choice of boxes to attack. Sarah is getting some very nice boxes from the man from Amazon, I wouldn't be interested in what's in them, but she says it's a bit like having a birthday.

I bet she misses me pouncing on her bed at all hours of the day and night, not to mention keeping it warm for her.

She is still sofaless but has two armchairs and her rocking chair. I hated it anyway, as it made me feel giddy when it moved, but she likes it, so that's fair enough.

Celia of course is my faithful friend, always loving and caring and anticipating all my needs, in fact, sometimes she recognises my needs even before I know I have them! That's because she is a cat whisperer, unlike Sarah who vacillated between whispering and shouting, mostly shouting. Which of course got her nowhere!

Sarah said she misses me throwing myself at her feet for a tummy rub, I have mentioned this to Celia, but I don't think she feels inclined to throw herself onto the floor and roll onto her back, but I will remind her before her next visit.

Oh yes about the *mousealeum*, I am still attempting to fill it *singlepawded*. I caught a whopper of a mouse, which Dave removed very quickly. I will have to see if I can catch a nice juicy one for Sarah's next visit.

I wouldn't want her to think 'Out of sight, out of mind,' but I will try to give her a reserved welcome, if I remember.

Sarah really is the limit, fancy googling 'cat's bum tea towel holder.' Even more amazing that when she looked it up, it actually came up with what she wanted. She was struggling with where to put her tea towel in her new kitchen, and tucking it into the handle of a drawer became an annoyance to her, as whatever she wanted was in the cupboard below it and that meant she had to move it somewhere else yet again. I really feel like telling her where to stick her tea towels, but my dignity wouldn't stoop to such a low ebb. I feel mortally offended and wondered how many times she had looked at me exiting a room and thought of that.

When she came around yesterday, I was out mousing, such a lovely thing to do on a sunny afternoon. She and Celia considered their idea of shopping for a mop and bucket and dustpan and brush much more fun, but I don't think so, there they were, cooped up in shops instead of enjoying the sunshine and what benefit would they gain from it. A friend rang Sarah on her return journey and asked a similar question. 'What are you going to do with a mop and bucket?' 'Waiting for Celia to come and use it!' was her droll reply.

Please note Celia will not be mopping Sarah's wet room. I wonder why it's called a wet room? It sounds very uncomfortable I can't think of anything I would want less in a house.

Surely, houses are to keep dry in? Sarah says it's so large she could almost throw a party in it, but I can't think of anyone who would want to come. She avoided saying 'it's big enough to swing a cat in,' which was very considerate of her.

She hadn't solely come to visit me which I consider another offence, she had planned to spend the evening doing sums, but just before they got here, she remembered she had forgotten her laptop. Some people use any old excuse to dodge their responsibilities and I understand that today she couldn't remember where she had put the potatoes for her tea. At least she didn't have to keep moving the tea towel as it is now firmly shoved in its appropriate place. Her words not mine.

As promised, I did find a large juicy mouse and left it on the doormat, was she grateful?

What, do you think? Having come in to show her, I was swiftly sent back outside only to find the mouse had gone, but it was cowering behind the drainpipe. I was so engrossed in trying to reach it that I never got to say goodbye.

I have no doubt that she will be back, you know what they say 'she will turn up like a bad penny,' hopefully with her laptop this time, no offence to Penelope Ashby. I don't mind her turning up as she always makes a fuss of me.

# September 2020

Shock, horror!
What will Sarah do when my book is published?

# 9th September

Goodness me, Sarah seemed very bouncy and positive when she came to see me.

As soon as she set eyes on me, she got down onto the floor and rubbed my tummy.

She doesn't do that to Celia so I think it must be a special thing she does with me.

Once down she proceeded to chat to me. The last time we spent together she said that she had got something exciting to tell me. I have been waiting with bated breath and not like I mentioned on the 31st March where I used the word baited as in attractive to mice. You can only hold your breath for so long and today I can breathe again.

Enough waffling.

Sarah said 'I have signed a contract to have your diary of daily lockdown *mewsings* published.'

My flabber has never been so ghasted, 'and you will be on the front cover, but don't get too big headed or your head won't fit through the cat flap.' She always meters out wise advice, but I usually ignore it because that's what cats do.

I am sure there must be a cat somewhere who doesn't fit into the stereotypical mould, but I haven't come across one yet!

'I need to take a good photo of you for the cover and press releases,' Sarah continued, looking mildly pleased with herself to be the bringer of such good news.

Gosh what a surprise, my mind racing ahead to appearing on the Graham Norton Show, Woman's Hour and Good Morning Britain. Sarah who seems able to know what I am thinking thought my dreams were a bit fanciful and pompous, but you can but dream and as she has previously quoted C. S. Lewis said, 'You are never too old to set another goal or to dream a new dream.'

She qualifies by being old, so this quote is very apt for her.

Of course, she would have to go with me for any interviews, although Woman's Hour is done on Skype.

Now the title of my book is a matter of great concern as she needs to get people's attention with it.

I suggested, 'The Amazing Diary of a Wonderful Cat', 'A Cat's Lowdown on Lockdown.' Or 'I'm the Cats Whiskers.'

Sarah suggested 'The Covid Diary of Phoebe Furnackerpan – lockdown and shielding with a naughty but nice cat.'

I have great sympathy with the royal family, with the paparazzi pursuing them all hours of the day and night. Armed with her camera. She followed me for the rest of the afternoon.

She even rolled about on the grass with me. Her friend Margaret used to get very embarrassed when Sarah would lie down on the ground to get a good angle, and always in a public place. She would shout, 'No Sarah, no Sarah, stop it, just stop it.' That was until Margaret took her to Beachy Head and as Sarah neared the edge of the cliff she shouted 'Lie down Sarah, please lie down.'

# 28th September

The bad penny has turned up again, she arrived with a bag bulging with stuff but nothing for me.

I noticed the camera was still joined to her at the hip.

I was so pleased to see her, I forgot to be offhand or even *offpaw*, and bounced up to her with such enthusiasm, she was speechless at such a rapturous welcome.

I didn't mean to let her know I was missing her, but my actions spoke louder than *meows.*

She has come to stay for a couple of nights, to do sums and keep Celia amused. I would have thought I was more than enough company, but then what do I know?

I had told you previously that she seemed transformed when doing sums but I am afraid that she has reverted to her previous dreadful self, with shouting and bad words.

So disappointing. I skedaddled off before a screwed-up ball of paper hit me. I hate to paint her in such a bad light, but I feel the need to be truthful.

I have been exemplary in behaviour and generosity, even taking Celia a mouse one night to her bedroom, alas like Queen Victoria she was not amused.

Sarah said it was a good job that Celia wasn't asleep with her mouth open or I might have popped it in there. I wouldn't object to someone dropping something delicious into my mouth but in Celia's case, I'm not so sure that it would be well received.

My friends have been calling around to play, to compensate for Sarah not being here as much, we have had some lovely times in the garden, and Ruby or Rosy have even ventured into the house, only into my bedroom of course. I can never tell which cat is which, as Rosy and Ruby are twins.

It was such fun the other day, when Celia walked in expecting me to be relaxing in my super-duper bed, I don't know why she even thought that I would be, as she knows I would rather sleep anywhere else.

The other night I insisted on lying on a bag full of more plastic bags, much to Celia's annoyance, she muttered something unintelligible about what a lucky cat I was, and that she had bought me such a lovely bed from T K Max. Anyway, there in my bed was one or other of the twins, giving the impression that it was the perfect place to sleep.

Humans are strange, Celia spends all her time telling me what a lucky cat I am, reenforcing the fact that I have a comfy bed to sleep on, but when I let one of the twins try it out, she shooo's them out of it, faster than you can say, 'J.K.Meowling.'

I really don't understand her, Celia that is, not J.K.Meowling, who Celia says writes wonderful stories, I think Sarah could do with some advice from her.

Back to Celia. I have tried to be more comforting and kinder, since Sarah has gone, I even sat on Dave's outstretched legs when he was relaxing in the breakfast room with his feet up on the coffee table, I'm not allowed to put my feet on any table but he is. Sarah who happened to be passing through, immediately pulled out her camera and took a few photos.

I didn't think they were very good especially as Dave's feet appeared much larger than me, Sarah said it's all to do with the angle she took it from, and that's exactly how she wanted the photo to look.

She said she is editing my book to get it ready to be printed. So, I had better be nice to her too.

Opposite her flat lives a tuxedo cat, who reminds her of Eric Morecombe, I have no idea why? She has called him Eric, it's something to do with him wearing top hat and tails.

I suppose she will come again soon, but if she makes a video call on the portal Celia always grabs me and tries to get me to wave and say hallo. It's so embarrassing, I am *purrfectly* capable of making my own decisions on who I bestow my royal wave on. If I wanted to join in the conversation I could climb onto her lap, but of course I wouldn't, being contrary, I would climb onto the table or somewhere else I'm not supposed to go and wait for them to notice me.

Sarah says she has got to draw a line under my diary, I do hope it's a straight one but I doubt it will be. If she doesn't do it my book will never get published.

The end of August seemed a good idea, (hers not mine) but I managed to squeeze in a few September ones.

My outpourings will still appear on my Facebook page 'Phoebe Furnackerpan' from time to time and on my website www.acatsatonic.

I hope I will see you there.

# Acnowledgements

I want to take this opportunity to thank all my friends, actual and virtual, who have encouraged me to find my voice and then been prepared to listen.

# Also By Sarah Veness

*The Memory Box*

A charming collection of illustrated short stories by an award-winning author, The Memory Box is a great gift for those who are carers or living with memory loss. The simple narratives encourage activities which can reawaken past memories, bringing the welcome relief of calmness and peace, in a sometimes confusing world.

Printed in Great Britain
by Amazon

65014580R00179